Writing
Essentials

A NORTON POCKET GUIDE

Dawn Rodrigues

NORTH ADAMS STATE COLLEGE

Myron C. Tuman

UNIVERSITY OF ALABAMA

W • W • NORTON & COMPANY

New York • London

The text of this book is composed in ITC Stone Serif and Helvetica with
    display set in Rockwell.
Composition by University Graphics, Inc.
Manufacturing by Courier Companies.
Book design by Jack Meserole.

ISBN-0-393-96933-9 *Writing Essentials*
ISBN 0-393-10072-3 *NT Connect for DOS + Writing Essentials*
ISBN 0-393-10073-1 *NT Connect Word for Windows + Writing Essentials*

W. W. Norton & Company, Inc., 500 Fifth Avenue, New York, NY 10110
    http://web.wwnorton.com
W. W. Norton & Company Ltd., 10 Coptic Street, London, WC1A 1PU

6 7 8 9 0

CONTENTS

Mechanics

ACKNOWLEDGMENTS

The authors wish to thank the following teachers for their thoughtful reviews of the manuscript:

William Condon, University of Michigan
Chandice M. Johnson, Jr., North Dakota State University
Nancy Montgomery, Sacred Heart University
Laurence E. Musgrove, University of Southern Indiana
James Raymond, University of Alabama
Geoffrey Schmidt, Illinois Valley Community College
Alison Warriner, Sacred Heart University

Writing Essays Online

1 Thinking, Writing, and Computers

Behind all writing is the writer's interest in altering, if only slightly, some preexisting understanding or condition of the world. (Indeed, some would argue that interest in change lies behind all thinking.) Even a simple letter home emerges from such an interest—possibly the practical interest in asking for money or the less immediate interest in informing family members about our activities or in attaining the feeling of comfort that goes with reaffirming our roots and sense of belonging.

Ideally, a natural connection exists between interest in writing and the unity of text. Something spurs you to write, and the writing you produce is linked by this concern. That is, your text seems to develop from this concern.

In the real world, however, you often write not necessarily to express an interest in a topic, but to meet the demands of other people. As students, for example, you are regularly given writing assignments. But even when your writing is not directed by someone else, you may have little interest in the writing itself (for instance, when you write home to ask for money), or when your interest in a topic is strong but unfocused (for example, when you are outraged by a rate increase proposed by the local cable television company).

1a Thinking and the Writing Process

There is a close connection among interest, thought, and writing—for example, your being surprised about a cable-TV rate hike, having angry thoughts about the situation, and writing a letter of protest. In both thinking and writing, you use a common vocabulary organized into a grammatical system to express ideas. You think with words, and you express your thoughts when you write. Nevertheless, there is a fundamental difference between the two. In thoughts, words and associations come and go quickly, without much order or opportunity for development; in writing, your goal is to get everything—words, thoughts, examples, and so forth—in logical, linear order: first things first, with everything else in its place, one item after the other, until the end. In a nutshell, thinking often seems easy; writing often seems hard.

The writing process bridges the gap between thinking and composing by encouraging writers to work through their topic in repeated cycles of prewriting and exploring, drafting and organizing, rereading, and revising. The hallmark of process-based writing classes is students regularly bringing drafts of their assignments to class for feedback from their classmates or teacher and then revising the pieces again for the next class.

1b Computers and the Writing Process

Computers offer an exciting new way to bridge this gap between thinking and writing. Words on a computer screen, while not as fluid as those in our minds, are not nearly as fixed as those on paper. When you write directly on paper or type, words are entered and stored on the paper at once. Thus, editing such a text in order to change anything you have already said requires considerable effort, usually rewriting or retyping. With word processing, the three acts of entering (and changing or editing), printing, and saving the text are separate. You still use the keyboard to enter what you want to say, but now text is recorded in the computer's memory and reflected on its monitor, allowing you to alter it at will and, later, to print and save it (technically, to issue commands that send the text—usually called a file—to a printer and to a disk for storage).

Because computers allow you to revise so easily what you have written (generally by deleting words or moving them from one location to another), you can take more chances with your ideas—try things out both during the initial thinking process and the drafting of an assignment. Indeed, writing with a computer is so fluid, in some ways so much like thinking, that the old categories of prewriting, drafting, and revising are no longer clear and distinct. Unlike traditional work, where each step takes place in a separate document, with word processing you can do all the work on a topic in a single file, deleting rough notes and early thoughts as the process proceeds.

1c Computers and Risk Taking

The writing process gives all writers the opportunity to go from an unformed feeling about a subject to its full expression in a text. The computer helps writers during this period of struggle and uncertainty by offering them considerable technical support. With just a couple of keystrokes, old work can be copied and safely stored, freeing you to revise your position or even to try a new approach to the same topic without fear of losing something. Likewise, there is less pressure to get everything lined up from the beginning. You can easily write the conclusion first or add something to the introduction at the end. Computers take some of the work and anxiety out of composition, enabling you to give writing some of the energy and spontaneity of thinking itself.

2 Prewriting

Methods for discovering and gathering ideas are often called prewriting strategies. **Prewriting** is a term used to refer to all the thinking, information gathering, and topic exploration that you do before you plunge into a first draft.

2a Exploring the Assignment

The best time to develop a risk-taking attitude is while thinking through the assignment. Most college writing will begin with a teacher-generated task that either defines your topic for you or instructs you to find a topic on your own. In either case, the assignment may also specify conditions about your audience and about your purpose in relation to that audience. Rarely, however, will a teacher be able to specify what it is about the topic that you find personally engaging.

Begin your work, therefore, by defining the assignment—especially in terms of topic or content, audience, and purpose—all the time seeking for ways to strengthen your interest in this topic.

2b Group Discussion

Probably the most valuable form of prewriting is the easiest one—talking with others. By telling someone about your topic or discussing topic ideas with others, you have a chance to

Exploring the Assignment

THE TOPIC
- What does the assignment ask me to do?
- What aspect of the topic most interests me? Why?
- What should the finished product look like? Does the assignment call for a certain genre or format such as a standard essay or research paper, letter to the editor, or editorial, or is it discipline-specific, calling for a format such as a proposal, memo, or lab report? How long must it be?
- Do I know enough about my topic?
- What do I need to learn?
- Where will I be able to gather information—books, magazines, online sources, talking to others?

AUDIENCE
- Who are my most likely readers?
- What do I know about my readers?
- How familiar are my readers with my topic? What are their probable opinions?
- What do I need to learn about my readers?
- Where can I gather information about my readers?
- What impact would I like to have on my readers?

PURPOSE
- What is the purpose of the assignment?
- Why am I considering this topic?
- What am I expected to accomplish by writing this?
- What do I want to accomplish by writing this?

think through what you want to say before you begin to write. The "Online Tip" on page 6 offers suggestions for discussing your ideas online.

2c Prewriting with Computers

This section below describes a number of practical, well-tested classroom techniques, all involving computers, for transforming your initial interest in a topic into writing that is both controlled and forceful.

BRAINSTORMING **Brainstorming**, a problem-solving technique, involves the spontaneous generation of ideas about a subject. To brainstorm, create a list of everything that comes

---

ONLINE TIP

Exchange Ideas in an Online Group Discussion

Computer facilities in most schools are now networked, and if the right software is available to your class, you may be able to discuss assignments with your classmates electronically.

The most common form of such software is electronic mail (E-mail), a program that allows you to write messages to one or more people you identify in the "To" field of your message or to one or more groups, called distribution lists since they automatically send your message to a list of individuals. Your class, for example, might be set up as a distribution list. Mail messages can be printed or exported to regular text files that can be read and edited with a word processor.

---

into your mind about your subject. Write it all down as quickly as you can in the order that you think of it. To push yourself, set a time limit for yourself, such as ten minutes, or a number of items, such as fifteen.

Subject: The Information Superhighway
The Internet
Prodigy and America Online
Interactive TV (allowing such things as ordering clothing like that
      worn by the characters on a show)
E-mail (even E-mail to the White House)
Staying in touch with high-school friends through E-mail
Writing to people from all over the world on E-mail
Searching electronic encyclopedias
Reading the newspaper on Prodigy
Accessing weather information
Courses offered online
Movies available through interactive TV
Effect of these changes on society

CLUSTERING   Brainstorming is just a start. After you have finished brainstorming, consider using another prewriting strategy, clustering, to organize your ideas. **Clustering**, a technique for grouping similar items together, helps you collect your ideas and focus your thinking.

Read over your brainstorming list, and consider how related items could be grouped together—that is, clustered. Begin by looking for items similar to the first item on your list. Put a "1" beside those items that match this item. Go to the next item on your list that does not have "1" beside it, and put a "2" next to it. Now proceed through your list, putting a "2" beside each similar item. Keep running down your list, using new numbers for items that do not fit into any existing clusters.

The Information Superhighway 1
Prodigy and America Online 2
Interactive TV (allowing such things as ordering clothing like that
   worn by the characters on a show) 3
E-mail (even E-mail to the White House) 1
Staying in touch with high-school friends through E-mail 4
Writing to people from all over the world on E-mail 4
Searching electronic encyclopedias 4
Reading the newspaper on Prodigy 4
Accessing weather information 2
Courses offered online 4
Movies available through interactive TV 3
Effect of these changes on society 5

So that you can see the results of your clustering, use MOVE BLOCK commands on your word processor to move the items into common groupings. Add new items and create new clusters, if you need them. Give each cluster grouping a name. (You don't have to use all the items that appear on your brainstorming list. It is unlikely that all of your first ideas will fit into your paper.)

CLUSTER #1: GOVERNMENT INVOLVEMENT

The Information Superhighway
E-mail (even E-mail to the White House)

CLUSTER #2: SERVICES CURRENTLY AVAILABLE

Prodigy and America Online
Accessing weather information
Video games such as "Where in the World Is Carmen
   Sandiego?" (*new*)
E-mail and bulletin boards for Prodigy users (*new*)

CLUSTER #3: INTERACTIVITY

Interactive TV (allowing such things as ordering clothing like that
   worn by the characters on a show)

Movies available through interactive TV
Voting on presidential debates and other issues (*new*)

CLUSTER #4: USES OF E-MAIL AND THE INTERNET

Staying in touch with high-school friends through E-mail
Writing to people from all over the world on E-mail
Searching electronic encyclopedias
Reading the newspaper on Prodigy
Courses offered online

CLUSTER #5: IMPLICATIONS

Effect of these changes on society

ONLINE TIP

Use Brainstorming and Clustering to Generate and Organize Ideas

Use the Move Block function of your word processor to group similar items from your brainstorming list into clusters. With the CAPS LOCK key depressed, type a heading or title for each cluster, and then use the Move Block function again to rearrange entire clusters in logical order—for example, from most to least important or from most to least obvious.

FREEWRITING AND NUTSHELLING **Freewriting** means what the name implies: totally free writing, done without worrying about grammar, typing and spelling errors, paragraphing, or coherence. Write about anything at all or, if you have a specific assignment, about anything related to that assignment. Write for a specified time period, such as fifteen minutes, or until you have written a page or more.

After you have finished freewriting, read over what you have written, and summarize your ideas in a **nutshell sentence**, one that captures the gist of what you were trying to say in your freewriting.

Here is a sample of some freewriting done on the subject "The Information Superhighway and Interactive Television":

I keep hearing about the Information Highway and interactive television. Every time I watch television or read the newspaper I try to figure out whether what is being talked about is good or not. I wonder if we'd use interactive tv all that much. I don't think people want to stop watching their regular nightly shows.

I've read about ways people will be able to take courses through interactive tv and play games with people from all over the world. I'm just not convinced that many people will want to change what they already do. I could see using Prodigy or something like it for checking on the weather and even for reading the newspaper. I just don't see how it will be useful to have something like this on a television set.

After each freewriting session, read over what you have written and write a summary or nutshell sentence. For example:

I doubt that interactive television will change people's viewing habits.

ONLINE TIP

Freewrite While You Draft to Generate New Ideas

Freewriting is especially productive with a computer because it is so easy to freewrite at any time during the writing process. If you are in the middle of a draft, trying to work out a particularly troublesome paragraph, just press ENTER a few times and begin freewriting right there—in the middle of your draft. If you come up with usable sentences, you can incorporate them into your draft by blocking and moving the text.

INVISIBLE WRITING   The point of **invisible writing**, or "writing blind," is to free writers from the urge to evaluate and revise their writing as they draft and to encourage them to let their ideas flow. You can try invisible writing at the computer, by turning down your monitor contrast (see page 10), or with pencil and paper. To work with paper, you will need two sheets of notebook paper, one sheet of carbon paper, and a used-up ballpoint pen. Place the carbon paper between your two notebook pages. Use the empty ballpoint pen to do your writing. Although you cannot see what you are writing as you write, when you look at the second notebook sheet—the one beneath the carbon paper—you will see the results.

Invisible Writing

Invisible writing at the computer is freewriting with your monitor contrast turned down. To try invisible writing, turn down the brightness control so that the screen is completely dark. Type without stopping for fifteen minutes or so. Then read over what you have written to see if there is an idea, a phrase, or a particularly good sentence that you can use in your draft or develop further using one of the other prewriting strategies.

PAIRING COMMON AND UNCOMMON **Pairing common and uncommon** is a prewriting strategy that can help you get started with the introduction, the conclusion, or the body of your paper. It may also help you organize your entire essay. (See "Contrasting Attitudes," page 15.)

First, list what is commonly known about your subject—typical opinions and well-known or obvious information, including what less-informed students are likely to think about this topic. Then, list what is *not* commonly known about your topic—information that your readers are not likely to know or understand. In addition to settling on a topic for your essay, you may be able to use your list in your introduction, conclusion, or body paragraphs.

COMMON KNOWLEDGE ABOUT THE INFORMATION SUPERHIGHWAY

> People have heard of the information superhighway.
> They read about mergers between telephone companies and cable companies.
> People have heard of Prodigy and America Online.

UNCOMMON KNOWLEDGE ABOUT THE INFORMATION SUPERHIGHWAY

> My readers may not have looked at Prodigy or America Online.
> My readers may not know that shopping services are already available on interactive TV in some parts of the country.

Taking the time to list the common and uncommon aspects of your topic helps in another way: by listing what you imagine your readers think about your topic, you are developing a heightened sense of your audience.

ANSWERING QUESTIONS **Answering questions** is a prewriting technique that can be adapted to any topic. In the following list of questions, just substitute your topic for the bracketed areas—[ ].

1. How is [ ] commonly defined? Do my sources define [ ] differently? How am I defining [ ]? What are the major parts of [ ]?
2. What things appear similar to [ ], and how are they different from [ ]? What things that appear different from [ ] are nevertheless similar?
3. How does [ ] develop? What are the origins of [ ]? What conditions affect the growth of [ ]? What is the purpose of [ ]?
4. What do people in general have to say about [ ]? What do experts have to say about [ ]? What is my personal experience with [ ]?
5. What are the conditions that make [ ] possible? How might those conditions be changed?
6. What do my readers know about [ ]? To what extent do I have to explain [ ] to them? How does their knowledge of [ ] affect the organization, style, and tone of my paper?

ONLINE TIP

Create a Prewriting Question Template File

A template file is a "master file" that you create for repeated use but do not actually write in. To create a prewriting question template file, save a set of prewriting questions as a separate file. Then, as you begin generating ideas for a draft, make a copy of the file with a new name, and write your answers to the questions directly into the new file. For example, a prewriting file using the common/uncommon strategy might look like this:

COMMON/UNCOMMON
1. Common views of my topic
2. Uncommon views of my topic

2d An Exploratory Draft

An **exploratory draft** is another means of discovering ideas. This draft, usually written before you have ample notes or a working outline, may be no more than a reflection of your random thoughts. Focus on putting your ideas into words, not on figuring out exactly what you want to say or where you want

---

CHECKLIST 2

Prewriting Online

ON YOUR OWN
- Brainstorm ideas, or freewrite anywhere in your file.
- Select a prewriting assignment file that your teacher has made available.
- Create reusable prewriting files with your favorite prewriting questions.

WITH ACCESS TO E-MAIL OR COLLABORATIVE SOFTWARE
- Share any brainstorming or other lists you have generated with classmates by posting that work to the network.
- Read what classmates have suggested in their prewriting exercises, responding to their work through additional messages to individuals or to the group.
- Revise your original prewriting effort and repost it to classmates.
- Copy helpful comments from classmates into your word-processing file using the Block/Cut/Paste or Import features.

the paper to go. You can work on these and other organizational matters after you finish your exploration.

3 Organizing the Main Ideas

How do you move from prewriting to drafting? Much depends on your writing habits and preferences. Many writers see the writing process as an opportunity to think through the writing task in order to arrive at a full and often complex statement of their ideas and their opinions. Some writers prefer to plunge in with an exploratory, or discovery, draft—an extended, focused freewriting session that will need extensive reworking. Other writers prefer to write a carefully structured rough draft, using an outline to guide them as they write. Before you begin your structured draft, however, you should settle on a working thesis statement and do some preliminary planning.

If you have written one or more exploratory drafts or if you already have a clear sense of purpose and organization, you may be ready to produce a **rough draft**—a draft in which you lay out your ideas in a unified, well-developed, coherent essay. You can revise as you write, but when you have finished your "rough draft," it should be clear to a reader that you have taken time to work through your ideas. Thus, your rough draft should develop a clearly defined thesis statement in an orderly way with supporting paragraphs.

3a Formulating a Thesis Statement

A **thesis statement** is a sentence or group of sentences that presents the main idea, or the focus, of an essay. It is an assertion or opinion in need of explanation, support, or development—a position about the world that readers are unlikely to accept without elaboration or proof. View your thesis statement as a promise to your reader that your essay will develop the topic in the way that your thesis statement implies.

The thesis statement in college essays is often the last sentence of the introductory paragraph. To formulate a thesis statement, examine your prewriting for ideas that might grow into a focusing statement—if your word-processing program allows it, possibly with the prewriting in one window and a draft of your paper in another. Aim to establish a working thesis statement that will help to channel your thinking before you begin drafting, but do not feel obligated to use that sentence in your actual draft.

Sample Working Thesis Statements

FIRST TRY   The services made possible through the Internet promise to change communication patterns in the home, at school, and in the business sector. One of the changes is the development of interactive television.

SECOND TRY   Technology, the Internet in particular, is changing the nature of television.

When should you write your thesis sentence? Some teachers recommend that students identify their thesis early in their writing processes. However, just because you have written a clear thesis statement does not mean that this is the topic in which you are genuinely interested. The best advice is to formulate a thesis early in your writing process but revise it regularly as your essay takes shape.

3b An Organizing Plan

Ideally, the organization of an essay should grow out of your thesis, the individual parts of your essay each representing a sensible means of developing the principal point you are making. If your organization does not follow your thesis, you have the option of reorganizing your major sections or reformulating your thesis.

With regard to organizing essays, it is important to realize that highly original, sophisticated essays can be based on simple, straightforward organizational plans in much the same way that dazzling houses can have simple floor plans. Indeed, one way to build something noteworthy is to start with a sound, uncomplicated plan. The two organization methods described below offer a means of forming an unlimited number of essay structures.

ENUMERATION   **Enumeration** entails listing items in numerical sequence: "first," "second," . . . "last." An essay that is organized this way develops its central idea through a series of paragraphs, each paragraph supporting a point or subpoint of the thesis statement. Effective use of enumeration will indicate what steps or stages you need to go through to show the true complexity of your topic. In particular, whenever you enumerate steps to work through in your essay, ask yourself the following questions (if you cannot answer "yes" to each of them, you may need to change the structure of your essay by reformulating your thesis or, more likely, reworking the steps you will be covering):

1. Is each of your points distinct, or are some merely restatements of others? A section on interactive television of the future, for instance, is likely to overlap with separate sections on the benefits and difficulties of interactive television.

2. Are your points roughly parallel, each point covering a comparable amount of material (for example, a section on television as it was, changes in television today, and prospects for television in the near future)? If it turns out that you are much more interested in one point than in the other two, try working that point into your thesis and seeing if you can divide it into a series of new points.

3. Are the points presented in a sensible order—from first to last, least to most important, or, like a relay team, with the weakest link in the middle?

4. Do all points, taken together, accurately represent your overall position on your topic? If not, then ask yourself what your points taken together do represent, and reword your thesis accordingly.

CONTRASTING ATTITUDES An essay developed by using **contrasting attitudes** supports its thesis by playing the common against the uncommon in the introduction. If, for example, you want to argue that interactive television will not change the way people watch television, you could begin by noting the common view—that technology has radically changed the lifestyles of Americans over the twentieth century—and then continue, in your thesis statement and in the development of your essay, by noting the uncommon attitude—that people may prefer to be passive observers of TV, not active participants. You could also use the common/uncommon structuring principle to present the opposite view—first noting in the introduction that people will do all of their shopping and communicating over interactive TV, then taking the position that interactive TV will be the end to our sense of community outside of the family room.

The overall structure of an essay based on the common/uncommon method of organization will vary, depending on whether you want to focus exclusively on either the common or the uncommon view of your topic or whether you want to devote the first few paragraphs of your essay to the opposing viewpoint before turning to your side of the issue. Again, your position may be the common one or the uncommon one. In the first few paragraphs of your essay, however, you may want to explain that you understand why some people hold a different view.

COMBINING ENUMERATION AND CONTRASTING ATTITUDES The techniques of enumeration and contrasting attitudes can be combined in most essays. The thesis that interactive TV will be part of our lifestyle might be developed by enumerating several reasons for your belief, each of which might be developed further by discussing some variation of contrasting attitudes. For example, at one point in your larger argument about the exciting possibilities of interactive TV, you could include several paragraphs that present the opposing argument—people might not want to interact with their television sets. Then you could move back to your main argument, perhaps to a paragraph that discusses how interactive TV will allow for new forms of political involvement via community forums. Even this strategy could be expanded by enumerating the ways in which interactive TV may change our lives constructively.

3c A Working Outline as a Drafting Aid

To provide some structure during your drafting sessions, consider creating a minimal, flexible outline with your word processor. Instead of using fixed, numbered headings and subheadings, type an informal list, and rearrange the items as your draft develops. Indent to add subheadings and details. As you write, you can freely add, delete, review, or move entire outline sections.

ONLINE TIP

Use an Idea-Generating Outline as a Drafting Tool

Create an idea-generating outline template such as the one below. When you draft your essay, first split the writing screen. Merge a copy of the outline template into one window, and put your drafting file in the other. Use your informal outline to get started, but allow yourself the freedom to alter your ideas as you write. After a few hours of drafting, revise your outline to match the current shape of your essay.

SAMPLE OUTLINE TEMPLATE
Introduction and Thesis:
    Key Idea:
        Supporting Points:
    Key Idea:
        Supporting Points:
    Key Idea:
        Supporting Points:

3d Paragraph Structure

The flexible combination of enumeration and contrasting attitudes, discussed above, also provides the basis for effective individual paragraphs. Like essays, most paragraphs should have a topic (called a **topic sentence**) and supporting information arranged in a logical way. A topic sentence (not always the first sentence) gives the reader some indication of what the rest of the paragraph will cover and may also provide the reader with a clue as to how the material will be developed. In this paragraph, for instance, the second sentence gives you an indication of the paragraph's topic.

Try to develop paragraphs that coincide with the purpose of your essay. For example, an essay explaining the importance of selecting the right college might include different kinds of paragraph patterns. One topic sentence might state that public universities and private colleges provide students with vastly different experiences; this paragraph would be developed best by using a contrasting-attitudes pattern. If, later in the same essay, you want to isolate some key differences between these schools, use an enumeration paragraph.

4 Framing the Main Ideas

Three key parts of an essay—the title, introduction, and conclusion—should work together to frame or support the organizing structure discussed in section 3. The introduction prepares readers for the thesis, the conclusion announces the end

Drafting Strategies

• Develop a working outline from the ideas you have generated in early freewriting or prewriting activities. Use your
outline to guide you as you make your draft. Don't limit
yourself, however, to the ideas in the outline. Remain
open to fresh insights and thoughts that occur to you as
you work. If your outline is on computer, you can easily
revise it to conform with any new direction your writing
is taking.

• Read over your emerging draft regularly, especially when
you start a new drafting session. Rereading both refreshes
your memory about the content of your text and gives you
a sense of how you need to adjust the evolving structure.

• Begin anywhere to get started—the end, the middle, wherever you want. Don't feel that you have to write your essay
in the same order that readers will read it.

• Try using the concepts of enumeration and contrasting attitudes to help you when you reach blind alleys while making a draft. Ask yourself, "Can I add a parallel example or
illustration in the next paragraph?" Or "Do I want to introduce a contrast to what I have just written?"

of the essay's development, and the title gives readers a handle
to the whole thing.

4a The Introduction

The introduction is your opportunity to capture your readers'
attention and interest them in what you have to say. It is important to think about your readers before you begin to write
and to keep them in mind throughout the writing process.

An effective way of introducing a piece of writing is by estab-
lishing some common ground between you and your readers,
leading up to your singling out one aspect of this common
ground that needs closer study or reconsideration—the thesis
statement. Some writers like to wait until after they have finished a draft to write an introduction; other writers find that,
having written the introduction, they have established sufficient momentum to write the rest of the essay. Although you

will want to create an introduction that fits your topic, at times you may find it difficult to get started. If you get stuck, try the common/uncommon prewriting strategy or see the sample introductions, below.

Sample Introductions

CURRENT ATTITUDES   State what most people think, followed by the thesis statement.

> ➤   Most people think of TV as a place to watch soap operas or basketball games. They turn on the set, expecting to sit back and relax. . . . [*Thesis*] Interactive TV is about to change these attitudes.

POSSIBLE SOLUTIONS   State alternatives; then suggest one solution as the thesis statement.

> ➤   What will be the most popular use of computers in the future? Some people say it will be E-mail; others, surfing the Internet for odd pieces of information. . . . [*Thesis*] Many will be surprised to learn that the most popular use will be a new mode of television.

DIRECT ANNOUNCEMENT   Simply say, "The paper is about. . . ."

> ➤   [*Thesis*] Interactive television will change everything you have ever thought about television or computers. . . .

QUESTIONS   Start with a question or a series of questions, followed by the thesis statement.

> ➤   What do you think is the most exciting thing about television today? Is it a group of guys sitting around watching the Super Bowl? Is it teenagers tuning in to the premier of new videos on MTV? . . . [*Thesis*] In the future, the most exciting thing on TV will likely be something quite different: people talking back to what they are watching.

ANECDOTE   Start with a brief anecdote, followed by the thesis statement.

> ➤   It is 3:30 in the afternoon, and Jonah is home alone after school watching television. Only he is not sitting still in front of the set the way kids used to. Every few minutes he. . . .

[*Thesis*] Jonah is taking part in what may well be the major new entertainment and information medium of the twenty-first century: interactive television.

ALLUSION   Start with a reference to another work, followed by the thesis statement.

> In Orwell's *1984*, there are television screens and television cameras everywhere. Regardless of where Winston Smith goes, ... [*Thesis*] Interactive television promises to be as intrusive in our lives, if less threatening.

DEFINITION   Start with a definition, followed by the thesis statement.

> Television is such a popular and pervasive medium that it seems unnecessary to define just what it means. Almost since its inception, however, the notion of broadcast has been at its center. . . . [*Thesis*] Interactive television is about to change what we mean by television.

UNRELATED FACTS   Start with a series of facts, followed by the thesis statement, which promises to pull those facts together.

> All the latest video games are still on the shelves at Toys "Я" Us. Not a soul is in JC Penney. The movies are deserted; the mall, empty. . . . [*Thesis*] Everyone is at home viewing interactive television.

QUOTATION   Start with a brief quotation, followed by an explanation of the quotation and a link to the thesis statement.

> A government official once referred to television as the "vast wasteland," suggesting a place of endless space and little content. This might have been an accurate description of much of the television of the past. . . . [*Thesis*] Interactive television may convert this wasteland into a virtual amusement park.

4b The Conclusion

A strong conclusion commonly restates your thesis, in different language or from a fresh viewpoint, and then widens the implications and scope of the thesis. An effective conclusion will often echo the introduction. One advantage of having a distinctive introduction—for example, beginning with the image of interactive television as a virtual amusement park in the "wasteland" of television, or of television cameras following Orwell's Winston Smith—is that you have something strong and colorful to return to at the end of your paper—an image of the exciting "rides" one may find on interactive television, or of a contemporary, less gloomy Winston Smith zapping Big Brother with the remote control and surfing the latest music channels. Thus, such references to the opening give readers a sense of completion.

What you should not do in the conclusion, however, is introduce new topics.

4c The Title

While some writers like to come up with a title before they write their essay, it may be more helpful to wait until you have finished a draft and have an effective opening. The best places to look for a title are in the opening and concluding sentences of your essay. Ideally, the title, the introduction, and the conclusion should all work together, and when you come up with a good idea for one, you can often extend this idea to include the other two. A paper on interactive television that begins with a reference to the "vast wasteland," for example, could play with this image—for example, "Reclaiming the Wasteland," if you are positive about the new technology, "The New Wasteland," if you are not.

Good titles should be brief, informative, and engaging. An acceptable title for a paper on the problems of developing the information superhighway might hint at both positive and negative features: "The Information Superhighway: The Promise and the Reality." The title becomes more engaging with a colorful allusion, "The Information Superhighway: Remembering the Yellow Brick Road," and perhaps more effective still when shortened to "Information Highway or Yellow Brick Road." Either title with a reference to the Land of Oz could then provide material for both your introduction and conclusion.

If you get writer's block whenever you try to think of titles, consider starting a "Title" file, in which you jot down title ideas that occur to you at any point during your writing course.

ONLINE TIP

Idea Files

Setting aside special files can help you organize and keep track of information you consult frequently as you write. Create the files below, or come up with variations of these to suit your purposes.

"GREAT IDEAS" FILE
Use this file to tuck away ideas that might be useful in the essay you are currently working on or that might fit into another essay.

"TITLES" FILE
Use this file to collect titles that fascinate you. Include good titles written by others as well as those you dream up yourself.

"ERRORS" FILE
Each time you have a paper returned to you with errors indicated, put the errors into this file for future reference. And remember to correct the errors in the file, too. Look at the file when you revise your paper to avoid making the mistake again.

"INTRODUCTIONS" FILE
Collect interesting introductions that you might use as models for your own work, or save introductions you have written that you especially like.

"CONCLUSIONS" FILE
Collect interesting conclusions that you might use as models for your own work, or save conclusions you have written that you especially like.

5 Revising

Revising is an important part of the writing process. Even though you may do a lot of revising while you draft with a word processor, your initial goal should be to generate a draft. When you have decided that your draft covers what you want to say, then you may focus on revision. Be sure to allow some time between completing the first draft and revising it; if you begin revising too soon, you may be too close to your material to be able to look at it critically.

5a Revising on Your Own

Read your paper thoughtfully, imagining that you are a naive but interested reader, one who has no specialized knowledge about your topic but who is eager to learn. If you print your draft, draw lines through sentences that need to be deleted. Draw arrows to indicate where you want to move paragraphs so that they are at their most effective locations. Insert new sentences to make your ideas flow smoothly. If you are revising directly at the computer, be sure to save your file with a new name before you begin to make changes. Instead of drawing arrows and marking sections for later revision, use the Move Block function to experiment with rearranging paragraphs, sentences, and words.

If you do most of your revision at the computer, you may want to print out and revise a version on paper as well. Reading in a different medium can help distance you from your ideas so that you may see your work more objectively and revise more effectively.

On-Your-Own Revision Questions

* Where would a reader get lost?
* What do I need to change to make my ideas clearer for a reader?
* Where do I need to create new paragraphs? If I create new paragraphs, do I need to make changes to the newly created paragraphs?
* Can my reader follow the movement of paragraphs? (*Note:* If not, try adding transitional sentences or phrases to guide the reader.)
* Do my paragraphs connect directly with my thesis statement?
* Do the sentences in each paragraph flow smoothly from one sentence to the next? If not, I will need to do some revising. (*Note:* Sometimes you can make sentence-by-sentence changes; other times you may need to recast an entire section. You can press ENTER a few times and do some trial revising in your document.)
* Is each paragraph adequately developed? If not, I may need to do more research to gather sufficient information. (*Note:* When you do have the information, move your cursor to wherever you need to add that information, and start typing.)
* Would a different introduction or conclusion strengthen my paper?

5b Group Workshopping

At some point in the writing process, all writers benefit by being able to share their work with others and, if possible, to read what others have written on the same or a comparable topic. While students can share their work informally outside of class, many teachers hold revision workshops in their classes. The most important aspect of such workshops is the opportunity it offers you to read your classmates' work and, thus, to get a better sense of what goes into writing an effective paper.

Group-Workshop Revision Questions

OVERALL
- Which paper(s) do you like best?
- Why?

INTRODUCTIONS
- Which essay has the most effective introduction?
- Why?

THE MAIN IDEA
- Which essay has the most compelling main point?
- Can you state this point in one sentence?
- How does your sentence match the thesis sentence in this paper?

COHERENCE AND ORGANIZATION
- Which paper makes it easy for you to follow the main ideas?
- Can you identify the parts of the paper?
- Can you identify any techniques the writer uses to move smoothly from one section to another?

CONCLUSION
- Which essay has the strongest conclusion?
- Why?

OTHER CONCERNS (AUDIENCE, SENTENCE STRUCTURE, EMPHASIS, ETC.)
- Are there other noteworthy aspects of any of the other papers that should be mentioned?

All papers have strengths and weaknesses, yours included. But in any group of papers, one or more will stand out as being more effective than the others. Always try to read at least three of your classmates' papers, and then ask yourself which ones work best and why? What, if anything, do these papers accomplish that could help you in revising your own paper? Which ones have a clear thesis and sense of development? Lots of compelling details? Good transitions? The most interesting title and introduction? The best conclusion? Use the questions in Checklist 5 to guide you.

If you have the opportunity, share your thoughts with your group, constantly seeing if you can detect reasons for the amount of agreement or disagreement within the group. If you don't have this opportunity, use what you have discovered to revise your own work, trying to make yours more like what you found in the most effective papers.

ONLINE TIP

Group Workshopping

If the software on your school's network allows you to share files, you can take part in group-workshop or peer-review sessions at different times of the day or week.

1. Save your work to the network so that it is available to your classmates.
2. Bring up each of your classmates' papers on your screen. If you are working in a group, read all of the papers on which you are supposed to comment.
3. Split the screen, and open a new window in which you can write. Using the revision questions in Checklist 5, comment on the papers as a group, being critical but kind and helpful. When you are finished, either print out your comments and share them with the group, or, if possible, post your comments to the network so that others can view and respond to them.

5c Peer Editing

In peer editing, you are to closely read another student's paper. As with group workshopping, it is always helpful to focus on what your partner needs to do to improve his or her paper. As a peer reader, phrase criticism carefully, remembering to be kind and helpful. Begin your comments with a compliment to the student whose paper you have read. Focus on questions of content and organization, saving minor points, such as grammatical errors, for last. (Better yet, postpone talking about grammatical and typographical errors until a later session.) Use questions such as those in Checklist 6 to guide you.

Peer-Editing Revision Questions

OVERALL
* What do you like best about the essay?

INTRODUCTION
* Do the opening lines of your partner's essay engage you?
* Why or why not?

THE MAIN IDEA
* What is the point of the essay?

COHERENCE
* Are there any places where you get lost?
* Can you suggest a revision?

ORGANIZATION
* Are the paragraphs well developed?
* What would you like to see expanded in the essay?

CONCLUSION
* Does the conclusion summarize or point forward?
* Can you suggest improvements?

OTHER CONCERNS (AUDIENCE, SENTENCE STRUCTURE, EMPHASIS, ETC.)
* Are there any other aspects of this paper that work well?

5d Copyediting and Proofreading

When you have revised your paper to your satisfaction, you need to take time for final editing (called copyediting) and proofreading. While you are revising your paper, you will make whatever changes you can to improve your writing. When you have done all that you can, you must then concentrate on locating and correcting mechanical and typographical errors.

Make sure you go through your paper several times, each time reading for one of the following purposes:

- To check paragraph structure
- To check sentence structure and sentence errors
- To run a spell check and to read to check spelling
- To check typographical errors
- To check word choice and usage

A word of caution: Do not substitute the use of a spell checker for a thorough proofreading. Spell checkers will not pick up usage problems or words that are mistyped but are still words (such as *he* for *the*). Also, read your paper in different media—several times on-screen and several times on paper. Errors that go undetected in one medium are often easy to spot in another.

ONLINE TIP

Editing and Proofreading Online

- Use computer error-checking tools cautiously. Many word-processing programs have grammar and style checkers built in to help you as you revise. They are less reliable than spell checkers, flagging items that may be correct while missing other problems.
- Check sentence and paragraph structure by moving the cursor through each paragraph one sentence at a time. Press ENTER if you find that you have shifted topics and may need a new paragraph. (You can return to this spot later and make a final decision.)
- Use your word processor's Search option to help you locate those places that you have marked on your printed draft and want to change on the screen.
- Use your word processor's Search function to locate instances of a particular kind of usage error, such as confusing *to*, *too*, and *two*, or *they're*, *their*, and *there*. Search for each word, and check to see if you have used it correctly. To correct an error, just type in the change.
- Run your paper through the spell checker, but remember that spell checkers do not catch all errors. Read your paper carefully before you turn it in.
- Proofread online by starting at the bottom of your file and reading backward, one sentence at a time, so that you do not get caught up in the flow of your ideas.
- Change the font of your paper on-screen or view it in a preview mode to make your paper look different and to help you spot errors.

Research
Writing

6 Planning a Research Project and Gathering Information

A research paper, like an essay, solves a problem or presents a point of view and, like an essay, needs to be planned, organized, and developed. Most of the prewriting, revising, and editing strategies suggested in the previous chapter can be used for writing research papers. Although some essays require the same kind of information gathering that is used in research papers, there are differences between writing a research paper and writing a personal essay. When writing an essay that draws largely upon personal knowledge, you can often formulate a thesis relatively early in the process. When writing a research paper, you may not be able to come up with a thesis until after you have done considerable background reading, note taking, and synthesizing of information. The information you do use in your research paper must then be documented. **Documenting** involves referring to, or "citing," the books, magazine and journal articles, newspapers, interviews, and so forth, that support the assertions you are making. Documenting the results of original research may also include presenting **visuals**—charts, tables, diagrams, and so on—to support your claims.

Different disciplines have different systems of documenting references and various formats for presenting the results of research. You will need to check with your instructor to find out which system you should use in your papers. The two most common forms of documentation are covered in this book: Modern Language Association (MLA) format used in English and the humanities and American Psychological Association (APA) format used in the social sciences.

6a Standard References and Indexes

Before you conduct a search, take time to get acquainted with your topic, using standard references, bibliographies, or specialized indexes. Gathering information for a research paper requires you to develop powers of detection—ways of searching for information, evaluating the sources of that information, and taking notes on the material so that you can use it efficiently as you write your paper. Information gathering can also involve interviewing friends and relatives on your topic, conducting surveys, and employing other research techniques.

Libraries are usually your first stop for published information. Look for information on your topic in references and indexes, electronic card catalogs, and online indexes (databases). You can also use selected areas of the Internet to explore your topic.

STANDARD REFERENCES   Whether you use your library or the Internet, begin by consulting such references as the *Oxford English Dictionary* or *Webster's Third New International Dictionary of the English Language* for definitions of any unfamiliar terms. You might also want to consult the *World Almanac and Book of Facts*, the *World Book Encyclopedia*, or *Grolier International Encyclopedia* for background information on your topic. These sources provide summaries of the general information that many educated readers may already possess and can be used to increase your own knowledge. As a rule, your status as an expert will be enhanced if, in your writing, you cite specialized sources, rather than general ones.

BIBLIOGRAPHIES   You may want to begin your reading by consulting one or more sources listed in an index such as the *Bibliographic Index*, which gives entire bibliographies on your topic.

PERIODICAL INDEXES   The term *periodical* refers to magazines, journals, and newspapers, which are often published on a regular basis, such as daily, weekly, or monthly. **Periodical indexes** are lists of articles published in particular fields. Below is a list of some periodical indexes:

Art Index
Book Review Index
Business Periodicals Index
Education Index
Humanities Index
New York Times Index
Readers' Guide to Periodical Literature
Social Sciences Index

6b Online Indexes

If you have access to **online indexes** (often called **data-bases**), you can conduct an electronic search. Your library may have electronic versions of some of the standard indexes; it also may have some indexes that have no print equivalent, such as ABI/INFORM, a business index. Some online indexes that might be available to you include the following:

EAI (Expanded Academic Index)—formerly InfoTrack
ERIC (Education Resources Information Center)
MLA Index (Modern Language Association Index)
ProQuest—a periodicals index covering the humanities, education, and the social sciences
SCIN (SciSearch—Science Citation Index)
SSCI (Social SciSearch—Social Science Citation Index)

6c The Online Card Catalog

Many libraries have replaced with electronic catalogs their large cabinets containing individual cards that represent each book in the library. These electronic catalogs are arranged by author, title, and subject.

To search effectively, try to identify the key terms (sometimes referred to as **descriptors**) used by librarians to catalog books and journal articles on your subject. The *Library of Congress Subject Headings* (LCSH) lists many alternate topics that might contain information on your topic and includes the pertinent Library of Congress **call numbers** (the identifying characters assigned to materials to indicate where in the library these resources may be found). Using carefully chosen search terms leads to more productive results. For example, if you are looking for material on the information superhighway, you would use the terms "information" and "superhighway." As you read through the results of your search and notice that interactive television seems to be an interesting topic, you might then want to conduct another search in which the words "interactive" and "television" have been combined.

6d The Internet

The **Internet** is a worldwide communication network that links computers at schools, colleges, businesses, and other sites. The Internet includes collections of information put together by faculty and students at different schools, by government officials, by social service agencies, and, increasingly, by specific businesses or industries. Other sources of information on the Internet are the many discussion groups, or **newsgroups**, where people from all over the world exchange ideas on an astounding range of topics. The groups themselves are organized under the name **Usenet**.

If your school is connected to the Internet, you can use the network to locate information such as government documents, discussion groups, electronic journals, library catalogs, as well as complete texts that are in the **public domain** (works without copyrights or with expired copyrights). Current works protected by copyright law (including practically all books and journals published in the last seventy-five years) are unlikely to be available free of charge.

SEARCHING THE INTERNET Traditionally, the major way to find information on the Internet has involved connecting directly to another computer by using a program called **Telnet**, and copying the files directly back to your computer, a process referred to as **file transfer protocol**, or **FTP**. The development of the World Wide Web makes finding, moving to, and copying this material much easier (see section 6e, pages 34–35).

To telnet to a computer, you need to know the computer's address—either a numeric one, such as 110.191.1.11, or an alphabetic one, such as database.carl.org. You can access the Library of Congress as well as other libraries through Telnet or through many campus Gopher servers. (A **Gopher**, a system of menus, helps you get around the Internet. The Gopher system is made up of **Gopher servers**, computers that contain all kinds of information and are affiliated with a university, a company, or another type of organization, and **Gopher clients**, computers that run the Gopher menu software that accesses the servers' information.) To access LOCIS (Library of Congress Information System), telnet to "locis.loc.gov" (140.147.254.3). There you will see a menu for the Library of Congress Catalog Files, Federal Legislation, Copyright Information, Foreign Law, Braille and Audio Files, and a file of selected organizations. This system is available Monday through Friday, 6:30 A.M. to 9:30 P.M. EST; Saturday, 8:00 A.M. to 5:00 P.M. EST; and Sunday, 1:00 P.M. to 5:00 P.M. EST.

LC MARVEL (Library of Congress Machine-Assisted Realization of the Virtual Electronic Library) is a Gopher-based campus-wide system that provides information about the Library of Congress, such as facilities and services, reading rooms, copyright, services to libraries and publishers, and so forth, as well as many electronic resources accessible through the Internet. To do an online search of LC MARVEL, telnet to "marvel.loc.gov" (140.147.2.15), log in as "marvel." You can also access LC MARVEL and most Gopher servers via the World Wide Web.

6e   The World Wide Web

Increasingly, materials on the Internet—images, sound bites, even movies, as well as traditional documents—are being linked together as part of a gigantic information structure called the **World Wide Web (WWW)**. The World Wide Web is a set of **hypertext documents** housed on computers across the world. (Hypertext documents have "hot" spots where readers can click and move to related information on their own computer or on a computer at another location.) A program called Mosaic has greatly accelerated this process since 1993, by making it easy to move from resource to resource and, thus, in theory, to find helpful materials. With Mosaic or with more recent information browsers such as Netscape, information screens work as menus (usually referred to as **home pages** since they offer links to many other home places), with key terms highlighted. As a user, you click on a highlighted term that interests you, and you are moved automatically to this new entry.

New search engines on the WWW are easy to use. For example, your school may offer a program that brings up a home page of search engines—for instance, WebCrawler, managed by Brian Pinkerton at the University of Washington. The WebCrawler home page will have a blank box where you can type in any term. If you enter "Babe Ruth," a new screen will appear with half a dozen highlighted items, each a link to somewhere else. In this case, one is a link to the Vincent Voice Lab at Michigan State University. Clicking on this link will bring you to the Vincent Voice Lab home page and the option "General sound samples," Clicking here will bring up the list of sample voices—for example, George Washington Carver, Amelia Earhart, Florence Nightingale, and Babe Ruth, "dying of cancer talks about baseball (1947)." If this were a document, then clicking here would display it on the screen. Since it is a sound bite, it is stored in a file that would ordinarily be downloaded and played there, assuming the computer had the necessary sound card and speakers.

The ease with which one moves through the World Wide Web—from a computer lab at the University of Alabama to an index program at the University of Washington to a voice library at Michigan State University—all in seconds and without any real technical expertise, gives searching the Internet a gamelike appeal.

ONLINE TIP

Searching Online Sources

- Start with a broad topic, and find out how much information you can locate in your library on that topic.
- Develop a list of descriptors or search terms, and revise the list as you find terms that yield better results.
- Use *and* and *not* in your searches.
  - —Many programs allow you to use two words that are joined by *and* to limit your search to all the sources that contain both words. (For example, searching for *interactive and television* would produce a list of all the sources that contain both words.)
  - —To exclude certain kinds of sources, use *not* between your search terms. (For example, searching for *written and composition not music* would produce sources that are about written composition, not musical composition.)
- Scan the list of sources, and jot down new search terms that are like the "See also" references that often appear in abstracts and summaries.
- Search in various databases, using the same terms as well as any new terms that appear. You will know that you have exhausted your search when the sources that you have already seen continue to appear as the results of your search.
- For potential sources of information and for search terms, skim through key books and journals, and consult bibliographies listed at the end of chapters or in the appendixes.
- Learn how to use search tools such as Netscape or Web-Crawler on the World Wide Web.
- Learn how to create a **bookmark**, a program feature of many Internet browsers that allows you to mark material to which you may wish to return. First, as you search on the Internet, locate a set of sources for your project. Then indicate to the computer that you want to save the location in your program.
- Mail information that you locate through the World Wide Web to your E-mail address, and incorporate it into your notes. (Check your World Wide Web or Internet program for directions on mailing files to yourself.)

6f Note Taking

As your work on a research paper proceeds, you will need to consult different kinds of references at different times. At the outset, to gain background knowledge, you should select references that provide you with general information about your topic. Later, after you have a good overview of your topic, you will need to narrow your focus and will probably turn to specialized sources, all the while taking careful notes on what you have found and where you have found it.

Note-taking skills take time to develop. Follow the techniques listed below, and adapt them to your needs:

- Keep a careful record of every source that is even remotely promising. References that seem only tangentially related to your topic early in the research process may prove crucial in the future. You will have less trouble locating the source later if you have accurate bibliographic information.
- Evaluate your sources critically. Do not take notes on a source unless you are fairly certain that it contains the kind of information you need. As you read a source, particularly an Internet source, question the reliability: When was it stated or published? What biases or hidden persuasive techniques are at work? Many published articles are written by journalists who rely on other people's research, research that may or may not be fully cited. Does the article point clearly to its research sources?
- Develop an effective method for note taking. Some writers use research notebooks that are divided into several sections: one for logging research activities, one for taking notes, one for working up a bibliography, and one for idea generating and making rough drafts. Other writers use note cards for both notes and bibliographic information. You can adapt either the notebook or the note-card technique to your own needs, combining traditional note cards and notebooks with their electronic equivalents.
- If you use a three-ring binder with section dividers for your research notebook, then your notebook can include handwritten as well as computer-generated pages. You can insert into your notebook printouts of your research notes from your files.

Keeping note cards separate from bibliography cards allows you to sort notes without disturbing the bibliography-cards file. All you need to include on a note card is sufficient information to link the card with the more complete bibliography card: key words and the author or a brief title. Include personal reactions to your sources so that you can remember your own point of view about the information you have recorded.

You may be used to using note cards only to paraphrase, summarize, or record quotes from such sources as books and journal articles. You can, however, also use note cards to summarize interviews with experts and to jot down your own ideas and insights.

Note taking can be a significant contributor to improper attributions when you draft your paper, thereby possibly leaving you open to plagiarism. (See section 8f, ''Avoiding Plagiarism'' [pages 47–48].) If you prepare summaries and paraphrases while reading your sources, be careful to indicate with quotation marks the exact words used in the source. To ensure that you are truly paraphrasing, try writing down another's ideas without the source open in front of you.

ONLINE TIP

Electronic Note and Bibliography Cards

1. Create a template file for each master card. Samples of each are shown below. Customize them as needed to accommodate your sources. Since the cards are designed for a word processor, the space will expand as needed.
2. After you design the cards, use the Block Copy function of your word processor to make multiple copies of the text in the file.
3. Each time you use the file, save a copy of it with a new name so that you can use your original bibliography-card or note-card file for another project.
4. Head each note-card with a key word or words that represent(s) an important concept in the source. You can then search your file to find all the notes you have taken on a specific topic with the same key words. For example, if you are writing about problems in the legal

system and want to find all of the notes you have taken that include the key words "defense attorneys," search for all instances of "defense." By searching a file that contains all your notes, you will be able to find and reorganize your notes by copying all related items to a new file.

5. When you take notes, indicate the usefulness or value of each source in a section of your bibliography card; also indicate your personal reaction to the source on your note card.

Note Card

Key words:
Author or brief title:
Notes:
Personal response to this source:

Bibliography Card

Author(s)/editor(s):
Title:
Volume:
City/publisher:
Date of publication:
Value of this source:
(Include ways in which you can use this source to support your own view of the topic, specific points in your paper where you might incorporate material from this source, or just your general reaction to the source.)

7 Writing the Research Paper

A research paper is a report on *your* investigation of a topic and should present *your* viewpoint on that topic, not the viewpoint of one or more of your sources.

If you have kept your notes in a separate file and saved the file with a new name, you can write your draft in the same file you used for note taking. Or you could work with two files: your notes files in one window, your draft file in another.

7a Developing a Controlling Idea

Review your notes regularly with the aim of discovering a focus for your paper. (You may also want to refer back to section 4, "Framing the Main Ideas" [pages 18–22], at this point.) Your sources will often direct you toward a focus. For instance, you are preparing to write a paper on the information superhighway. After having read mostly favorable reports, you may find a source that is especially skeptical. That source could provide you with a controlling idea: proponents of the information superhighway stress its promises and opportunities rather than the potential problems it poses for society. As you continue exploring sources, you may want to begin focusing on the problems—determining the issues of contention and the reasons some people are more skeptical than others about the information superhighway.

Eventually, you will be able to narrow your focus still further and explore one aspect of your topic in greater depth. The sample paper on pages 48–53, for example, considers one aspect of the information superhighway: problems related to interactive television. If the purpose of your paper is to explore a topic in which you are interested—for instance, to learn about general problems of the information superhighway—then a broad topic may be acceptable. But you will still need a specific focus as a way of getting into and organizing the material you will have collected. Of course, you should get your teacher's approval before proceeding with your research.

7b Drafting the Paper

If your paper will be longer than three or four pages, plan to do some preliminary organizing before you begin drafting, and refer back to section 2d, "An Exploratory Draft" (page 12). Some writers develop outlines; other writers prefer to make informal lists.

When you are ready to draft, give yourself the time to write for a few days or weeks. Divide your topic into several parts, label each part, and work on each separately.

As you draft one section of your paper, you may come across information or think of ideas that you can use in another section. If you are drafting in the file with your notes, move to the top of your file, and create a new note card for your new notes.

Or move your ideas to the end of your file, and keep them there until you need them.

7c Revising Your Work

When you have finished drafting your entire paper, take time to revise it, referring back to section 5, "Revising" (pages 22–27). Many students find that after they have written their drafts, they must rearrange the material so that the paper says what they want it to say. One technique that can help is the **descriptive outline**. Read through your draft, and write descriptive labels on it—headings that accurately describe not what you wanted to say in each section, but what you actually have said. When you are finished, you should be able to look more critically at your paper and make your revisions. (See the sample paper on pages 48–53.) Remember to save a copy of your file with a new name before you write descriptive headings in it.

VIEWERS' INTEREST IN THE SERVICES

Will viewers want these services enough to pay for them? Viewers will be able to customize what they want to look at and what they don't. Viewers will be able to select the programs they want to watch, and they will be able to watch these programs in any order, at any time. If Mom and Dad want to read the *New York Times* on the electronic newsstand, they can do that while watching a nightly news segment that corresponds to the news item they are reading about, a segment that they will be able to locate by programming their television to find shows on a specific topic. If the children want to take a Japanese course, they can select that option. But if not enough people and schools are willing and able to purchase services such as these, the businesses that offer them are not likely to succeed.

RELIANCE ON ADVERTISING

Lee says that interactive television is likely to rely largely on interactive shopping to generate capital. "A consumer watching *Seinfeld* on a smart . . . TV decides that he wants to order a jacket like Seinfeld's so he clicks on it using a remote control. The show pauses and gives him the opportunity to buy the garment in a choice of colors and the jacket is purchased on the viewer's credit card which has already been entered into the TV" (81).

Here is a portion of the "descriptive outline," with a possible change noted, of an early draft of the research paper on pages 48–53:

Expense involved in building the information superhighway
Schools' lack of ability to purchase the services
Usefulness of services
Viewers' interest in the services
Reliance on advertising to pay for the superhighway

After reviewing the movement of the paper, the writer saw that the section about schools' lack of ability to pay for services would more logically follow the section on paying for home services. The writer moved sections around as she revised the paper.

8 Using Sources in Your Paper

Your finished research paper should reflect your ability to weave quotations and references to your sources into your own text. The sample research paper on pages 48–53 demonstrates effective ways of referring to sources in the text using parenthetical citations.

8a Documentation Systems

Documentation systems are standard ways that writers in a given field credit their sources by citing them in the text and listing them at the end of the paper. **Citations** are the references to sources that are placed in parentheses as close to the sources as possible. The "Works Cited" or "References" section is a bibliography of all works referred to in the paper.

Undergraduates are most commonly asked to use either of two citation systems: the Modern Language Association (MLA) or the American Psychological Association (APA).

If you have consulted only one or two references, you may be able to include the full bibliographic information directly in the text the first time the work is mentioned:

➤ As Eugene Provenzo notes in *Beyond the Gutenberg Galaxy*, we are only the "potential masters" of this new electronic technology (New York: Teachers College P, 1986, 95).

In both MLA and APA citation styles, when you refer to the author or the work in your sentence, do not repeat that information in the citation, either in a full citation like the one above or a partial reference to the complete citation at the end of your paper. Thus, Provenzo's name is not repeated in the citation. For more on in-text citation, see pages 57–62 and 72–76.

**C
H
E
C
K
L
I
S
T

7**

Sources That Must Be Cited

DIRECT QUOTATIONS
Quote directly from your source, if the original words are unique and distinctive or if they add authority to your point. At times, you may decide to include a direct quotation simply because the content of the original passage cannot be paraphrased without destroying the impact of the author's words.

IDEAS THAT ARE SUMMARIZED OR PARAPHRASED
You need to make clear to readers when you are summarizing or relying extensively on one or more sources related to your topic. You can do this in the text itself or in an explanatory note.

**IDEAS AND OPINIONS ASSOCIATED WITH A
PARTICULAR PERSON**
If you refer to specific concepts adhered to by one economist, such as John Maynard Keynes, you must include a reference to him. Otherwise, a reader might assume that you had created that economic theory yourself.

**DATA THAT, IN THE CONTEXT OF YOUR PAPER,
MAY BE OPEN TO DISPUTE**
If you cite statistics related to smoking among college students, you need to include a reference to your source.

**COMPILATION OF INFORMATION IN GRAPHS, TABLES,
AND CHARTS**
If you use information from a table or a chart, you need to cite it, even if you do not include the entire chart in your paper.

**RESULTS OF SURVEYS YOU HAVE CONDUCTED AS PART
OF YOUR RESEARCH**

QUOTATIONS OR SUMMARIES FROM INTERVIEWS

8b What to Cite

As you write, cite all information that is not commonly known about your topic. You must acknowledge (by placing within quotation marks) the exact words taken from another source, including any distinctive individual word or short phrase, and all individual sentences or strung-together phrases. You must also acknowledge the source of material you paraphrase: any distinctive ideas that you found elsewhere and are restating in your own words.

Exactly what to document will vary according to what information and expectations you can assume your readers have about the subject as well as what you have given your audience in your text.

8c Paraphrasing, Summarizing, and Quoting

Let your thesis provide the momentum of ideas in your research paper. Use quotations, summaries, and paraphrases to support what you want to say. Avoid stringing quotations together and expecting the reader to understand how they relate to your point. As much as possible, write paraphrases and summaries of your sources on your note cards, rather than using direct quotes. You will, however, want to record some quotations— especially if they express an idea succinctly—even if you are not sure that you will use them.

PARAPHRASE   A paraphrase is a restatement of a portion of text in your own words. The paraphrased text should follow the gist of the original source and should be roughly the same length.

> ORIGINAL   A new company called Catapult Entertainment recently introduced a video-game network service that would enable video-game players to compete against each other over telephone lines via a special Catapult modem (Peterson).

> PARAPHRASE   A company called Catapult Entertainment has just developed a video game for interactive television that would allow viewers from different parts of the country to play with one another (Peterson).

SUMMARY   A **summary** is a condensed version of a text, ranging from a short passage to an entire book or journal article, and should be much shorter than the original text. The following is a summary of a three-page article:

➤ Currently, the part of the information superhighway known as the Internet is free for educators and students who access it through college or high-school computers (Gilbert 3).

DIRECT QUOTATIONS   Direct quotations must contain the exact words of your source, as in the following:

➤ According to Lee, the task of wiring just the "private homes with the fiber-optic cable that will be necessary for such a quick exchange of high amounts of information could cost $100 billion" (82).

8d Placement of Parenthetical Citations

Parenthetical citations should provide readers with an immediate sense of how much of a text is the author's own and how much is based on other writers' work. Even though these citations do not provide comprehensive information, they should give readers enough data about the author and the title of the source to reduce the need to consult continually separate endnotes or the "Works Cited."

Place citations carefully to keep your own text uncluttered. Parenthetical citations are best placed at a natural pause in the sentence, preferably at the end. You can minimize the need for lengthy parenthetical insertions by providing as much information as possible in the text itself.

➤ As Eugene Provenzo notes in *Beyond the Gutenberg Galaxy*, we are only the "potential masters" of this new electronic technology (95).

8e Incorporating Source Information into Sentences

Introduce source information into your sentences naturally. Below are some suggestions for varying the style in which you incorporate quotations, paraphrases, and summaries:

1. Introduce the quotation directly.

➤ According to Lee, "Even wiring private homes with the fiber-optic cable that will be necessary for such a quick exchange of high amounts of information could cost $100 billion" (82).

2. Provide a connection to previous text before introducing a new citation, whether that citation is a direct quotation or a paraphrase.

> ➤ Jay David Bolter disagrees with Gilder. In *Writing Space*, he argues that people won't want to interact with their television sets (132). In Bolter's view, people are not used to interacting mentally when they watch television shows. They watch to lose themselves, not to think (132).

Note how the first sentence provides the connection between the previous text and the paraphrase in sentences 2 through 4.

3. Incorporate only a small portion of a quotation.

> ➤ Steven P. Schnaars, author of *Megamistakes: Forecasting and the Myth of Rapid Technological Change*, claims that "most technological forecasting over the past quarter century was dead wrong" (qtd. in Wilson 14).

4. Use ellipses (. . .) to eliminate irrelevant material from a quotation.

ORIGINAL QUOTATION	Technology is creating a world in which much of the traditional role of education institutions could be completely reshaped by the availability of information on command to individuals in and outside of classrooms, at times convenient to the learner, in forms far richer than classroom discussion, and in an order totally unrelated to a syllabus or course outline.
USE OF ELLIPSES	In an article in the *Educational Record*, Blenda Wilson points out that making information available "on command" could reshape "the traditional role of education institutions . . . in forms far richer than classroom discussion, and in an order totally unrelated to a syllabus or course outline" (9).

Note: Make sure that a sentence with ellipses reads clearly and correctly after the ellipses have been inserted.

5. Incorporate portions of direct quotations into paraphrases.

ORIGINAL QUOTATION   Consistent with this, we are moving toward a marketing universe-of-one, in which the individual consumer self-selects those messages from the companies with whom one wishes to do business.

PARAPHRASE   Martin Nisenholtz explains that interactive-television customers will choose "messages from the companies with whom one wishes to do business" (28). Viewers will be able to choose what they want to look at and what they want to ignore.

ONLINE TIP

Incorporating Sources into Your Paper

1. Most word processing programs allow you to open multiple documents in multiple windows. Open your note files in one or more windows and your document file in another.
2. Once you have done this, you can block and copy any notes or drafts from your note or draft files into your document.
3. Since it is always easy to delete electronic text, you can copy your notes directly into your document file (thus avoiding having to switch between two or more windows) and then use Move and Delete functions within this one file to get your document in the form you desire. Remember, you can delete your notes from your document and still retain a copy of them as long as you copied them originally from other files.

Note: Programs that do not allow for multiple windows will still permit you to open your document file and use a Merge function to look inside other files, block text there, and automatically copy it back ("merge it") into your original document.

8f Avoiding Plagiarism

The act of passing off as one's own the words or ideas of another is called **plagiarism**. The work you improperly pass off as your own can be that of a published author or of a classmate and, in both cases, either the actual words used by that person or that person's distinctive ideas. In all colleges and universities, passing off other people's words or ideas as your own is a serious violation of academic ethics and is grounds for severe penalty.

Dealing with summaries and paraphrases always remains a potential source of difficulty for student writers. (See section 8c, "Paraphrasing, Summarizing, and Quoting," pages 43–44.) Sometimes students will prepare summaries and paraphrases that very closely follow parts of the original source, including some direct quotations, but will neglect to add the quotation marks; then weeks later, when they compose their paper, they may forget just which words and phrases are their own and which come directly from the original source. Remember that when you take notes, you must put quotation marks around all direct quotations; and, to be certain that paraphrases and summaries are truly in your own words, you should write them without looking at the original sources.

Dealing with distinctive ideas is not as precise as dealing with exact words, and here a few guidelines are in order. It is often to your rhetorical advantage as a would-be expert to attribute specific ideas to specific people; one sign of being an expert yourself is knowing which other experts to cite. Within a normal class discussion, many ideas will be exchanged. Here, too, it is both ethically required and a sign of strong writing that you acknowledge in your text specific classmates as the source of specific insights. This is especially necessary if your class is using online workshopping and the regular sharing of papers— a situation that will also allow you to quote directly from classmates, an acceptable practice as long as you use quotation marks and acknowledge the source in your text. Check with your individual professors as to whether or not you should cite them as sources for ideas that they raise during normal class discussion. Your professors may possibly expect you to consider these ideas as belonging to the public domain of the class.

When you cite Internet sources, be sure to give credit, using the appropriate citation format (see pages 70–72 and 80–81). Respect the "intellectual property" of Internet authors: cite anonymous as well as authored sources. In addition, it is considered good etiquette to write to the author of an E-mail, newsgroup, or Listserv message and request permission to cite him or her in your paper.

Remember the general rule to cite all sources of distinctive or controversial information and to use direct quotations when citing other people's exact words, whether published or not. Finally, as a matter of style, try to resist the temptation to quote others extensively.

9 Sample Research Paper with MLA Parenthetical Style

Marsha Rollins

EH 309-002

Mr. Hebert

16 March 1995

The Information Superhighway: Possibilities and Problems

We hear about the superhighway daily on television and read about it in the newspapers. According to most sources, the information superhighway promises to change home life. But no one is sure what the information superhighway will really bring to the home and to the classroom. Tosca Moon Lee expresses many peoples' confusion about the superhighway in "The Information Interstate: Superhighway or Superhype?":

> It's here now. It's not here yet. It's cable t-v. It's fiber optic, 500-channel, full-video, couch-spud nirvana bulldozing virtual asphalt to a home near you. It's the information superhighway! . . . or is it? (80)

Video games, movies, and catalog products are available from the convenience of your armchair or classroom. All this sounds wonderful, but is it? In order to resolve our confusion, we need to look not only at the promise, but also at the problems.

Among the many offerings that interactive television promises to bring to the home are business services, interactive political discussions, and interactive games. Businesses are migrating to the Internet, sometimes hiring employees who work at home, using home computers to communicate with their employers and their customers. One company in Acton, Massachusetts, WORDNET, runs a translation service totally through the network (Webster 70). Other possibilities for interaction online include interacting with politicians after a debate, a feature already available on Prodigy and America Online (Kantrowitz and Rosenberg 60) and playing games with people all over the country. A friend of mine tells me that a new company called Catapult Entertainment recently introduced a video-game network service that would enable video-game players to compete against each other over telephone lines via a special Catapult modem (Peterson).

People will have more educational opportunities in the home and in school, too. They will be able to take classes without leaving their homes and send E-mail to people from all parts of the globe. And the information superhighway's computer networks could enable students to customize their own learning needs at school. In an article in the *Educational Record*, Blenda Wilson points out that making information available "on command" could reshape "the traditional role of education institutions . . . in forms far richer than classroom discussion, and in an order totally unrelated to a syllabus or course outline" (9). E-mail access lets students communicate with others interested in similar topics or collaborate on common projects. For example, through services such as KidLink and Prodigy, students are already taking part in joint projects with other students from all over the world.

Currently, the part of the information superhighway known as the Internet is free to educators and students who access it through college or high-school computers (Gilbert 3). Homes of today can access some of the resources of the information superhighway if they subscribe to services such as Prodigy and America Online, which customers can call up, using their computers and modems; and, for those families who can afford them, new TVs are being created that will be capable of accessing information services. Les Perelman goes so far to suggest that the Internet and interactive television will change the nature of education, since it will make it possible for children to receive instruction at home, not only in school (1993).

But all is not rosy. As more sophisticated services become available through the Internet, the Internet will become more costly to operate. More expensive networks will be needed. According to Lee, "Even wiring private homes with the fiber-optic cable that will be necessary for such a quick exchange of high amounts of information could cost $100 billion" (82).

Will viewers want these services enough to pay for them? Lee says that interactive television is likely to rely largely on interactive shopping to generate capital.

> A consumer watching *Seinfeld* on a smart . . . TV decides that he wants to order a jacket like Seinfeld's so he clicks on it using a remote control. The show pauses and gives him the opportunity to buy the garment in a choice of colors and the jacket is purchased on the viewer's credit card which has already been entered into the TV. (81)

Much of the success of the information superhighway depends not only on peoples' interest in making such purchases, but also in their willingness to do so.

People are only likely to purchase advertised products if they see them. Today's television makes it difficult to avoid advertising, but interactive television of the future may allow viewers to select only those programs or portions of programs that they want to view. Martin Nisenholtz explains that interactive-television customers will choose "messages from the companies with whom one wishes to do business" (28). Viewers will be able to choose what they want to look at and what they want to ignore:

> Advanced networks will create highly fragmented media markets. The consumer will have vastly increased choice and control over media options. The notion of consumers having access to 1500 channels is a misnomer; over time, the consumer will have access to and control over only one channel: his or her channel. And one will tailor that channel to suit one's needs and desires. (28)

If people do not choose those stations with the advertisements, then little revenue will be generated for continued superhighway construction.

People's current viewing habits do not fit the vision superhighway designers have for interactive television. People are couch potatoes, not active viewers. People will need to become more active viewers if interactive television is going to succeed. If interactive television develops programs based on using the television only to present information, then it will fail. But if the developers of new media take a different approach than that of television producers, they might succeed. George Gilder, the author of *Life After Television: The Coming Transformation of Media and American Life*, feels that interactive television should "appeal to people's special curiosities and hobbies and career interests . . ." rather than to their lower-level interests (35). Jay

David Bolter disagrees. In *Writing Space*, he argues that people won't want to interact with their television sets (132). In Bolter's view, people are not used to interacting mentally when they watch television shows. They watch to lose themselves, not to think.

Few schools have either the technology or the funding to purchase the services of interactive television. To access these technologies requires at least one phone line in every classroom. It also requires voters to approve school-bond levies so that schools have sufficient funds. Without funding, schools have to rely on voluntary contributions. Funding isn't easily gotten, and, if it is, there are other trade-offs. In Colchester, Vermont, for example, voters voted in the money needed to support technology in the schools; at the same time, they voted down a levy for higher salaries and health benefits for teachers (Wilson 12).

Looking at the problems along with the possibilities reminds us that we are only at the beginning of a major transformation in our society. The kinds of changes taking place will probably give way to newer advances. Will the information superhighway overcome the many problems and develop its potential? Steven P. Schnaars, author of *Megamistakes: Forecasting and the Myth of Rapid Technological Change* claims that "most technological forecasting over the past quarter century was dead wrong" (qtd. in Wilson 14). Some version of the superhighway is likely to make an impact on society, but just how extensive that impact will be remains to be seen.

Works Cited

Bolter, Jay David. *Writing Space*. Hillsdale, NJ: Erlbaum, 1991.

Gilbert, Steven. "Welcome to the Internet: Nightmare or Paradise?" *American Association of Higher Education Bulletin* 46.7 (1994): 3–4.

Gilder, George. *Life After Television: The Coming Transformation of Media and American Life*. New York: Norton, 1992.

Kantrowitz, Barbara, and Deborah Rosenberg. "Ready, Teddy? You're Online," *Newsweek* 12 Sept. 1994: 60–61.

Lee, Tosca Moon. "The Information Interstate: Superhighway or Superhype?" *PC Novice* Sept. 1994: 80–87.

Nisenholtz, Martin. "The Digital Medium Meets the Advertising Message." *Educom Review* 29.4 (1994): 27–30.

Perelman, Les. "School's Out: Hyperlearning, the New Technology, and the Shape of Education." *Wired Magazine* 13 Jan. 1993: 1.1 Online. America Online. 15 Jan. 1995.

Peterson, John. Personal conversation. 1 Oct. 1994.

Schnaars, Steven P. *Megamistakes: Forecasting and the Myth of Rapid Technological Change*. New York: Free P, 1989.

Webster, Bryce. "Global Input, Global Output." *Connect* Sept. 1994: 70–72.

Wilson, Blenda. "In Search of Progress in Human Learning." *Educational Record* 75.3 (1994): 8–16.

MLA and APA Documentation

In all academic writing, you must acknowledge sources of information, ideas, or words. This book describes two documentation systems: Modern Language Association (MLA) and the American Psychological Association (APA).

10 MLA Documentation

MLA style consists of in-text citations that refer readers to a list of works cited at the end of a paper.

10a In-Text Citation Format

- MLA citation requires two pieces of information, either in your text or in parentheses:

  1. The name of the source, usually indicated by the name(s) of the author(s)
  2. The page reference(s) in that source. If you are citing the entire source, you can omit the page reference(s)

- The source must be referred to in your citation or text in the same way that it appears in your "Works Cited."
- If the name of the author of your source is clear from your text, it should not be repeated in the parenthetical citation.
- The page number(s) can be omitted for a one-page article or a reference source arranged alphabetically.

> *Eulogy*, as defined by the *Harper Handbook to Literature*, is "a speech or composition of praise, especially of a deceased person."

CHECKLIST 8

ONE WORK BY ONE AUTHOR   If the author's name is not referred to in your sentence, include the last name and the page number in parentheses. There is no comma between the author and the page number.

> Although computers may lead to many improvements in education, critics contend that computers lack the ability to provide a "cure for ills that are social and political in nature" (Roszak 219).

> Although computers may lead to many improvements in education, computer critic Theodore Roszak contends that they lack the ability to provide a "cure for ills that are social and political in nature" (219).

> The advent of printing, writes historian Elizabeth Eisenstein, is of such importance because it led to "fundamental alterations in prevailing patterns of continuity and change" (2: 703).

Note: In a multivolume work, use a colon to separate the volume and page numbers: "(Eisenstein 2: 703)."

> You need to develop a sense of your readers' needs (Dobrin 104–09).

TWO OR MORE WORKS BY ONE AUTHOR   If you will be citing more than one work by an author, include a short form of the title, along with the page number(s), so that readers can tell to which work you are referring at that point in your text. If it is not clear from the context, begin with the author's last name, followed by a comma, then the title of the work, and the page reference.

> As a hopeful symbol of the modern age, the personal computer "supplies answers and restores composure" (McCorduck, *Universal* 284). The prospects for artificial intelligence, McCorduck concludes in an earlier work, are "nearly beyond comprehension" (*Machines* 357).

The complete title for the first reference is *The Universal Machine*; for the second reference, it is *Machines Who Think*. Remember to be consistent in your use of the abbreviated form of the author's work.

ONE WORK WITH TWO OR MORE AUTHORS   With two or three authors, include the last name of each author either in your text or in parentheses.

> ➤ The rapid spread of computer technology is leading to the "evolution of a new species, a species we have dubbed 'micro man' " (Pask and Curran 3).

With more than three authors, include the last name of the first author listed plus "et al." (an abbreviation of *et alii*, "and others").

> ➤ In revising an essay, writing experts contend, it is important to "attend to the major problems first" (Lauer et al. 284).

WORK WITH AN AUTHOR AND EDITOR   Clarify in your text (and enter accordingly in your "Works Cited") the person—editor or author—to whom you are referring.

> ➤ Culture allows us to reconsider with a critical eye what Victorian critic Matthew Arnold refers to as "our stock notions and habits" (6).

> ➤ In J. Dover Wilson's word, Arnold "shuddered" (xviii) at the lack of culture in nineteenth-century England.

CORPORATE AUTHOR   Cite a corporate author by its full corporate name, including, where possible, that name in your text as introductory material or, as a parenthetical insertion, at the end of your sentence.

> ➤ In his hearing before the United States Atomic Energy Commission, J. Robert Oppenheimer expressed "grave concern and anxiety" about the development of the hydrogen bomb (229).

> ➤ In his hearing to regain his security clearance, J. Robert Oppenheimer stated that the development of the hydrogen bomb was a matter of "grave concern and anxiety" (United States Atomic Energy Commission 229).

NO AUTHOR OR ANONYMOUS   Identify works without authors by title, using only the first word or words of a long title.

> ➤ *Moonbeam* advertises itself as a computer program to determine the "phase, position, and illumination of the moon."

"Moonbeam" is a shortened version of the title of an anonymous program.

AUTHOR QUOTED BY ANOTHER SOURCE Include "qtd. in" ("quoted in") before the name of your source.

> ➤ Sir Bernard Lovely notes that overly narrow and regimented computerized research in astronomy is damaging to "the free exercise of that happy faculty known as serendipity" (qtd. in Roszak 115).

AUTHORS WITH THE SAME NAME If a paper includes references to different works by authors who have the same last name, refer in your text to the first instance of the reference by using the author's complete first name and last name.

> ➤ In her article on computers in composition classes, Dawn Rodrigues notes that teachers should combine instruction in word processing with instruction in composition (3–4). In his article on teacher evaluation, Raymond Rodrigues stresses the importance of explaining teaching techniques to administrators (88–89). Dawn Rodrigues and Raymond Rodrigues agree that teachers should play an important role in teaching students the links between technology and writing.

If your in-text citation is fully parenthetical, however, you must add the first initial to the author's last name.

> ➤ In one article, on computers and composition classes, it is noted that teachers should combine instruction in word processing with instruction in composition (D. Rodrigues 3–4). In another article, on teacher evaluation, the importance of explaining teaching techniques to administrators is stressed (R. Rodrigues 88–89).

TWO OR MORE WORKS IN ONE CITATION Give the parenthetical citations to two or more sources as you normally would, separating the citations with semicolons.

By different authors

> ➤ Both agree that electronic mail is important (Hawisher and LeBlanc 3; Eldred 47).

The above example assumes that only one work by each author is included in the paper.

> ➤ Both agree that electronic mail is important (Hawisher and LeBlanc, *Electronic* 3; Eldred, *Mediating* 47).

This example assumes that the "Works Cited" includes more than one reference by each author.

By the same author

➤ The influence of computers on society is noted frequently in discussions of computers in instruction in writing (Selfe, *Situating;* Selfe, *Designing*).

This example assumes that entire works by one author are being referred to—hence, the shortened titles and no page references.

PART OF A SOURCE Include the page number and, when it does not appear in the text, the author's last name when referring to a specific part of a work.

➤ Although computers may lead to many improvements in education, critics contend that computers lack the ability to provide a "cure for ills that are social and political in nature" (Roszak 219).

PERSONAL COMMUNICATION Since readers will find it difficult to check the information contained in a personal communication, try to cite such references in the text. (Remember to list such references in the "Works Cited.")

➤ According to J. M. Thomas (personal communication, March 9, 1987), . . .

LITERATURE When citing a classical play, omit the page reference, and cite by section (act, scene) and line number, using either Arabic numbers or Roman numerals or a combination of both.

➤ In Shakespeare's *Hamlet*, Polonius advises Laertes to "give thy thoughts no tongue" (1.3.59).

➤ In Shakespeare's *Hamlet*, Polonius advises Laertes to "give thy thoughts no tongue" (I.iii.59).

Do not cite poetry by page. Instead, cite by section number (if appropriate) and line number, or, for poems without numbered lines, by title.

➤ In "Song of Myself," Whitman identifies himself with the "procreant urge of the world" (line 45).

For the last citation, use the word *line* or *lines* to prevent your reader from confusing *l.* and *ll.* with the numbers one and eleven. Once it is established that the numbers refer to lines and not pages, you can then cite the numbers alone.

THE BIBLE   To cite a book of the Bible, do not underline it or use quotation marks around it; follow it with the chapter and verse numbers.

➤ (Genesis 39.23)

Note: Ordinarily, you would include the Bible only in your in-text citation, not in your "Works Cited."

NONPRINT SOURCES SUCH AS FILMS AND RECORDINGS   In your text, cite the title and/or the name of the person chiefly responsible for that work, depending upon your own emphasis, and enter the complete reference to that work under the person's name in your "Works Cited."

➤ Cinematographer Nestor Almendros does some of his finest work in capturing the rural Texas landscapes in *Places in the Heart*.

ELECTRONIC SOURCES   Standards for citing electronic sources, such as online data bases, E-mail communication, and electronic journals, have just begun to emerge. Some privacy issues have not yet been clarified, such as whether you need to request permission from someone who has posted a message on a Listserv discussion group as you would be expected to do with personal correspondence (letters) or personal E-mail. We recommend that you acknowledge the source of direct quotations, the same as with other sources, by citing the author's name (if available) in the text and listing the full textual reference under that name in the "Works Cited." Note that with electronic sources there are no page references to include. Again, as with print sources, if the citation has no author, then refer to the title or some other identifying feature in both your textual citation and in the "Works Cited."

➤ Fifty years ago, Vannevar Bush predicted the appearance of "wholly new forms of encyclopedias."

➤ According to *The Chronicle of Higher Education*, Stephen King's new novel, *Insomnia*, was the third most widely read book on college campuses in its very first week ("What They Are Reading on College Campuses").

10b "Works Cited"

Starting on a new page entitled "Works Cited" and using the MLA style, list all the works you have cited—and only those you have cited. Treat each entry separately, putting the first line of each entry flush against the left margin and all subsequent lines of that entry indented approximately five characters or one-half inch from the left margin.

Arrange entries alphabetically by the author's last name or, when you have no author's name, by the first significant word in the title. When you have several works by the same author, list the entries alphabetically by title. Give the author's name in the first entry only; thereafter, use three hyphens followed by a period in place of the author's name.

ONLINE TIP

Bibliographic Tools

There are two kinds of software tools that can help you prepare a bibliography:

1. Some programs will format the bibliography for you—in either MLA or APA format. These programs will ask you to enter each piece of information as a field in a database and will then automatically format this information for you. The tricky part of such helpful programs is making certain that the data get printed correctly as part of your paper—with proper page number, header, and font.

2. Other programs will provide an online guide to bibliographic format as you enter your own entries, either as word processing text or in a separate part of the word processing program. Built into the word processing program, this kind of program will automatically alphabetize entries and place them in the proper format as well as take care of all printing concerns.

10c "Works Cited" Entries: Books

The main divisions for each book entry are as follows:

1. **Author**   Give the author's last name first, followed by a comma, then the first name, and a period.

2. **Title** State the book's full title, separating the subtitle from the title with a colon. Italicize (underline) the full title, and place a period at the end.
3. **Publication Information** Include the *place of publication*, the *publisher*, and the *date of publication*.

- If more than one city of publication is mentioned, give the first city of publication only.
- Shorten names of well-known publishers, omitting articles ("A," "And," "The") but keeping "UP" for "University Press" ("Norton," rather than "W. W. Norton & Company"; "Iowa UP," rather than "Iowa University Press").
- Use the latest copyright date if no date is given on the title page or "n.d." if no date is given at all.

The following are variations and/or examples of MLA bibliographic style for citing books.

BOOK WITH ONE AUTHOR AND/OR EDITOR

Lanham, Richard. *The Electronic Word: Democracy, Technology, and the Arts.* Chicago: U of Chicago P, 1994.

Tompkins, Jane P., ed. *Reader-Response Criticism: From Formalism to Structuralism.* Baltimore: Johns Hopkins UP, 1980.

BOOK WITH AN EDITOR'S MATERIAL Referring to editor's material only:

Wilson, J. Dover, ed. Introduction. *Culture and Anarchy.* By Matthew Arnold. New York: Cambridge UP, 1961.

Using a cross reference to refer to both editor and author:

Wilson, J. Dover. Introduction. Arnold xi–xl.

SECOND OR LATER EDITION OF A BOOK

Lauer, Janice, et al. *Four Worlds of Writing.* 2nd ed. New York: Harper, 1985.

Note: Other abbreviations commonly used for second or later editions are "rev." for "revised," "enl." for "enlarged," and "abr." for "abridged."

BOOK WITH TWO OR THREE AUTHORS OR EDITORS

Crawford, John C., and Dorothy L. Crawford. *Expressionism and Twentieth-Century Music*. Bloomington: Indiana UP, 1993.

Use the order of the names given on the title page, inverting only the first name.

BOOK WITH FOUR OR MORE AUTHORS

Lauer, Janice, et al. *Four Worlds of Writing*. 2nd ed. New York: Harper, 1985.

Give the name of the first author listed on the title page, and add "et al.," which stands for *et alii* ("and others").

BOOK OF TWO OR MORE VOLUMES

Eisenstein, Elizabeth L. *The Printing Press as an Agent of Change*. 2 vols. New York: Cambridge UP, 1979.

BOOK IN A NUMBERED SERIES

Wolf, Maryanne, Mark K. McQuillan, and Eugene Radwin. *Thought and Language/Language and Reading*. Reprint Ser. 14. Cambridge: Harvard Educational Review, 1980.

REPRINT OF A BOOK

Huey, Edmund Burke. *The Psychology and Pedagogy of Reading*. 1908. Cambridge: MIT P, 1968.

BOOK IN TRANSLATION

Turgenev, Ivan. *Fathers and Sons*. 1861. Trans. Rosemary Edmonds. New York: Penguin, 1965.

Begin the entry with the translator's name if you wish to cite the translator's introduction or notes.

Edmonds, Rosemary, trans. *Fathers and Sons*. By Ivan Turgenev. 1861. New York: Penguin, 1965. vi–xix.

Peterson's Competitive Colleges, 1995–96. Princeton: Peterson's
Guides, 1995.

Orwell, George. *1984.* 1949. New York: Signet Classic-NAL, 1961.

Dewey, John. *The Study of Ethics: A Syllabus.* Ann Arbor, 1894.

For books published before 1900, you may omit the name of
the publisher.

United States. Dept. of Labor. Bur. of Statistics. *Dictionary of
Occupational Titles.* 4th ed. Washington: GPO, 1977.

Orwell, George. "Why I Write." *The Orwell Reader: Fiction,
Essays, and Reportage by George Orwell.* New York:
Harcourt, 1956. 390–96.

Whitman, Walt. "Song of Myself." *The Norton Anthology of
American Literature.* Ed. Nina Baym et al. 4th ed. vol. 1. New
York: Norton, 1994. 2048–90.

Treat a published proceedings as a
book, but add all relevant conference information.

Harrington, Susanmarie, et al., eds. *Ninth Conference on
Computers and Writing: Lessons from the Past, Learning for
the Future.* Ann Arbor, May 20–23, 1993. Ann Arbor: U of
Michigan P, 1993.

Baym, Nina, et al. *The Norton Anthology of American Literature.*
4th ed. 2 vols. New York: Norton, 1994.

Whitman, Walt. "Song of Myself." Baym 1: 2048–90.

If you are using two or more works from a collection of works by various authors, list the collection by the name of its editor and use that for cross-referencing.

ARTICLE IN A COMMON REFERENCE WORK   If the articles are alphabetically arranged, omit the volume and page numbers. Start the entry by citing the author, using the initials, usually given at the end of the article, to find the author's name from the list of contributors at the beginning of the first volume. If the article is unsigned, start the entry by citing the article title. Don't give full publication data when citing a familiar reference book.

> Fieldhouse, David K. "Colonialism." *Encyclopedia Americana.* Int. ed. 1981.

> "Hayti." *Encyclopaedia Britannica.* 9th ed. 1875–89.

ARTICLE IN A SPECIALIZED REFERENCE WORK   For specialized reference works (usually those that have appeared in only one or two editions), give full publication information.

> Frye, Northrop, Sheridan Baker, and George Perkins. "Classicism." *The Harper Handbook to Literature.* New York: Harper, 1985.

10d "Works Cited" Entries: Articles

The main divisions for each entry of an article in a periodical are as follows:

1. **Author** Give the author's last name first, then the first name, and a period.
2. **Article** State the article's full title, separating the subtitle from the title with a colon. Enclose the full title in quotation marks.
3. **Publication Information** For an article in a scholarly journal, include the *name of the journal,* in italics (underlined); the *volume number;* the *year of publication;* and the *page references.* For an article in a newspaper or magazine, include the *name of the newspaper or magazine,* in italics (underlined); the *day* (if applicable), *month* (abbreviated), and *year;* and the *page references.*

The following are variations and examples of MLA bibliographic style for citing articles in periodicals.

ARTICLE IN A SCHOLARLY/TECHNICAL PERIODICAL   If each volume of a periodical is paginated continuously, then give only the volume number when citing.

> Broad, William. "Rewriting the History of the H-Bomb." *Science* 218 (1982): 769–72.

If each volume of a periodical is *not* paginated continuously—that is, each issue begins with page 1—then give the volume number, followed by a period and the issue number.

> Posèq, Avigdor W. G. "Soutine's Two Paintings of Pigs." *Source: Notes in the History of Art* 14.2 (1995): 38–46.

If an article does not appear on successive pages—if, for example, it begins on page 21, then skips to page 23, and goes on to page 25—cite only the first page, followed by a plus sign.

> Roberts, Steven K. "Artificial Intelligence." *Byte* Sept. 1981: 164+.

UNSIGNED ARTICLE   List unsigned articles by title.

> "Dispatch Case." *The Chronicle of Higher Education* 21 July 1995: 37.

ARTICLE IN A MAGAZINE OR NEWSPAPER

> Larson, Jennifer. "How Well Do You Know Your Drives?" *PC Novice* Aug. 1992: 17+.

For newspapers organized by sections, include either the section letter ("A," "B," "C," and so forth) directly before the page number ("A1+" or "D12") or the section number directly before the page number ("sec. 1: 5+").

> Eichenwald, Kurt. "Angry Chrysler Board Prevents Iacocca from Using Stock Options." *New York Times* 7 July 1995, late ed.: D1+.

Canby, Vincent. "The Heart of Texas." Rev. of *Places in the Heart*,
dir. Robert Benton. *New York Times* 21 Sept. 1984, late ed.:
C8.

Nelson, Lars-Erik. "The Rise of Russia's Criminal Class." Rev. of
Comrade Criminal: Russia's New Mafiya, by Stephen
Handelman. *Newsday* 9 July 1995, *FanFare*: 33.

If the review is neither signed nor titled, begin the entry with
"Rev. of," and alphabetize the entry under the title of the work
being reviewed.

10e "Works Cited" Entries: Other Sources

PERSONAL LETTER

Bernstein, Basil. Letter to the author. 18 June 1987.

INFORMATION FROM A DOCUMENT/DATABANK

Hawes, Lorna, and Barbara Richards. *A Workshop Approach to
Teaching Composition*. ERIC, 1977. ED 155 936.

If the source originates from a publisher other than ERIC (Educational Resources Information Center), give the original publisher's name and date of publication before the ERIC number.

SOFTWARE

Word Finder. Computer Software. Microlytics, 1986.

After the date, you may add other relevant information, such
as operating-system requirements.

TV/RADIO PROGRAM

"Rubinstein Remembered: A One-Hundredth Anniversary Tribute."
American Masters. Narr. John Rubinstein. PBS. WBIQ,
Birmingham, AL. 17 July 1987.

After the title of episode (if known) and program, give the names of those chiefly responsible for it.

RECORDING   Alphabetize recordings under whatever element you wish to emphasize the most, ending with the manufacturer and the year of issue.

> *Aïda.* By Giuseppe Verdi. With Birgit Nilsson, Franco Corelli, Grace
> Bumbry, and Mario Sereni. Cond. Zubin Mehta. Orchestra
> and Chorus of the Opera House, Rome. LPs. Angel, n.d.

> Bartoli, Cecilia. "Voi che sapete." By Wolfgang Amadeus Mozart.
> *Mozart Arias.* London, 1991.

FILM   Alphabetize either by film title or by principal individual.

> *Schindler's List.* Dir. Steven Spielberg. Perf. Liam Neeson, Ben
> Kingsley, and Ralph Fiennes. Universal, 1993.

> Spielberg, Steven, dir. *Schindler's List.* Perf. Liam Neeson, Ben
> Kingsley, and Ralph Fiennes. Universal, 1993.

PERFORMANCE

> *Misalliance.* By George Bernard Shaw. Dir. Tony Van Bridge. Perf.
> Nancy Boykin, Betty Leighton, and Kermit Brown. Alabama
> Shakespeare Festival, Montgomery. 4 July 1987.

INTERVIEW   To cite an interview that you conducted, include in the entry the name of the interviewee, the type of interview (personal, telephone), and the date.

> Goldberg, David. Telephone interview. 23 July 1995.

If the interview has been published or broadcast, give the relevant bibliographic information in the appropriate form.

> Kundera, Milan. Interview. *New York Times* 18 Jan. 1982, sec. 3:
> 13+.

ELECTRONIC SOURCES   "Works Cited" entries for electronic sources should include

1. **Author**   Give the author's name, last name first.

2. **Title** For articles, give the full title of the article or document in quotation marks. For full texts, italicize (underline) the title.
3. **Publication Information** Give the *name of the journal, newsletter* (include volume and/or issue numbers), *conference, or database.* Standards are still in flux, but your professor may prefer that, if one exists, the *title of the print analogue* appear before the *title of the electronic source.* Include *publication dates* and *page or paragraph numbers, print and/or electronic,* next to the appropriate source. Give the *publication medium* ("Online") and the *computer service or network* you used to find the source, as well as the *date* you accessed it. Finally, provide *availability information* for Internet sources.

Publication on diskette

Wresch, William. *Writer's Helper.* 3rd ed. Diskette. Ames: Conduit, 1993.

Publication in multiple media

Perseus 1.0: Interactive Sources and Studies on Ancient Greece. CD-ROM, videodisc. New Haven: Yale UP, 1992.

Online databases

Garrow, David. "On Race, It's Thomas v. an Old Ideal." *New York Times* 7 July 1995: E1. *New York Times Online.* Online. America Online. 28 July 1995.

Perelman, Les. "School's Out." *Wired Magazine* 3 Jan. 1993. Online. America Online. 28 July 1995.

World Wide Web

Bush, Vannevar. "As We May Think." Reprinted from *Atlantic Monthly* (July 1945). http://www.isg.sfu.ca/~duchier/misc/ vbush (9 Oct. 1995).

"What They Are Reading on College Campuses." *Academe This Week.* http://chronicle.merit.edu.bestbooks.html (9 October 1995).

Personal E-mail correspondence

> Kemp, Fred. ACW-L (Alliance for Computers and Writing List).
>   14 June 1994. Availability: listproc@ttuvm.bitnet.

Internet Listserv

> Rodrigues, Dawn. "Re: Open Discussion." 6 June 1993. Online
>   posting. Listserv MBU-L (Megabyte University). Internet.
>   28 July 1995. Availability: listproc@ttuvm.bitnet.

11 APA Documentation

APA style consists of in-text citations that refer readers to a list
of references at the end of a paper.

11a In-Text Citation Format

APA citation requires three pieces of information, which are
placed either in the text or in parentheses:

1. The source of the article, usually the name(s) of the au-
   thor(s)
2. The date of publication
3. The page number(s) in that source

If you are citing the entire source, you can omit the page numbers.

ONE WORK BY ONE AUTHOR   Include the author's last name
either in the text or within parentheses, separated by a comma
from the year of publication. Add a page reference if you are
referring to a specific part of a reference. Here are two rules to
keep in mind:

1. When including a page reference, make sure that the
   date is followed by a comma and that the abbreviation
   "p." or "pp." precedes the page number.
2. When you refer to the author, either in the text or in
   parentheses, use the *last name only*.

   ➤ Although computers may lead to many improvements in
     education, critics contend that computers lack the ability
     to provide a "cure for ills that are social and political in
     nature" (Roszak, 1986).

   ➤ Roszak (1986) discusses the limitations of computers to
     cure social ills.

C
H
E
C
K
L
I
S
T

9

The above format is often used when you do not want to cite specific pages.

➤ Although computers may lead to many improvements in education, one computer critic contends that they lack the ability to provide a "cure for ills that are social and political in nature" (Roszak, 1986, p. 216).

TWO OR MORE WORKS BY ONE AUTHOR   If you have two or more works by the same author, the year of publication is often enough to differentiate one work from another. If two or more works were written in the same year, distinguish among them by adding "a," "b," "c," and so forth after the year.

➤ Bruner, 1986a
Bruner, 1986b

If the above works were included in the same paper, "Bruner, 1986a" would refer to "Bruner, J. (1986). *Actual minds, possible worlds*"; "Bruner, 1986b" would refer to "Bruner, J. (1986). *A study of thinking.*"

ONE WORK WITH TWO OR MORE AUTHORS   With two authors, include the last names of *both* for all citations, using an ampersand (&) instead of the word *and* between the names. Follow the names with a comma and the date of publication.

➤ . . . not merely large calculators (Feigenbaum & McCorduck, 1983).

With three to five authors, give the name of each author for the first reference and, for subsequent citations, the name of the first author only, followed by "et al." ("and others") and the year.

FIRST CITATION

➤ Stanley, Shimkin, and Lanne (1988) argue . . .

➤ . . . (Stanley, Shimkin, & Lanne, 1988).

SUBSEQUENT CITATIONS

➤ Stanley et al. (1988) argue . . .

➤ . . . as has been argued (Stanley et al., 1988).

With six or more authors, use the last name of only the *first* author followed by "et al." for all textual references, but list all the authors in the reference list.

➤ But Jones et al. (1994) maintain . . .

CORPORATE AUTHOR   The names of corporate authors are usually spelled out each time they appear in the text. However, corporate authors with long names or with familiar abbreviations may be shortened after the first citation.

FIRST CITATION

➤ . . . AIDS research (National Institute of Health [NIH], 1988).

➤ . . . future plans (NIH, 1988).

NO AUTHOR OR ANONYMOUS   If a work has no author, cite in the text the first two or three words of the title, using quotation marks or italics (underlining) for articles and books, respectively; then give the year.

➤ Another source (*College Cost Book*, 1983) notes . . .

➤ As the *College Cost Book* (1983) notes, . . .

AUTHOR QUOTED BY ANOTHER SOURCE

➤ Lovely notes that overly narrow and regimented computerized research in astronomy is damaging to "the free exercise of that happy faculty known as serendipity" (as quoted in Roszak, 1989, p. 115).

AUTHORS WITH THE SAME NAME   If your reference list includes two or more authors with the same last name, include the authors' initials in all textual references, even if the years of publication differ.

➤ As R. A. Adams (1986) and P. B. Adams (1989) both contend, . . .

TWO OR MORE WORKS IN ONE CITATION   List the parenthetical citations to two or more sources in the same order in which they appear in the reference list—alphabetically. List two or more works by a single author chronologically.

➤ . . . appears promising (Feigenbaum & McCorduck, 1983; Roszak, 1989, 1991).

➤ Past research (Britton, 1972, 1985) . . .

PART OF A SOURCE   Include a page number or other appropriate reference when referring to a specific part of a work. Acceptable APA abbreviations for parts of a publication include "chap." ("chapter"), "No." ("Number"), "p." and "pp." ("page" and "pages"), and "Vol." ("Volume," as in "Vol. 2").

➤ Although computers may lead to many improvements in education, critics contend that they lack the ability to provide a "cure for ills that are social and political in nature" (Roszak, 1986, p. 219)

PERSONAL COMMUNICATION   Personal communication should be cited in the text but not in the References.

> ➤ Writing Across the Curriculum programs have not yet fully integrated technology (S. McLeod, personal communication, February, 1992).

ELECTRONIC SOURCES   In your text, acknowledge the source of direct quotations or distinctive material, providing the author's name, E-mail address, or some other identifying feature of the source (for example, name of Listserv, title of CD-ROM, and so forth).

> ➤ A key participant in the anthropology discussion list ANTHRO-L gives his opinions on the topic of race (Saundberg, 1994).

E-mail communication is treated the same way as letters and is cited in the text but not in the "References" section.

> ➤ Students enjoyed using E-mail in my English course. Sandra Smith explained that "it feels more like talking to classmates" (personal E-mail communication, June 15, 1995).

11b "References"

Starting on a new page entitled "References" and using the APA style, list all the works you have cited. APA recommends a "hanging indent" format for final copy, including student papers.

Arrange entries alphabetically by the author's last name or, when you have no author's name, by the first significant word in the title. When you have several works by the same author, list the entries chronologically, starting with the earliest publication. When you have several works by the same author with the same publication date, arrange the entries alphabetically by title and use the lowercase letters "a," "b," "c," and so forth after the year and within the parentheses.

11c "References" Entries: Books

The main divisions for each book entry are as follows:

1. **Author** Give the author's last name first, followed by a comma, then the initials.
2. **Date** Put the date of publication within parentheses.
3. **Title** Italicize (underline) the full title. Capitalize only

the first word of the title and subtitle as well as all proper nouns.

4. **Publication Information** Include the *place of publication*, then the *publisher*.

* When citing a publisher's location, give the city and state for U.S. publishers and the city and country for foreign publishers. If more than one city of publication is listed in a book, give the first one only.
* You may shorten the name of a well-known publisher ("Norton" instead of "W. W. Norton & Company").

The following are variations and/or examples of APA bibliographic style for citing books.

BOOK WITH ONE AUTHOR OR EDITOR Capitalize the first word of the title and subtitle, and any proper names; italicize (underline) the entire title.

Erikson, E. H. (Ed.). (1978). *Adulthood.* New York: Norton.

Lesser, G. S. (1974). *Children and television: Lessons from Sesame Street.* New York: Random House.

BOOK WITH TWO OR MORE AUTHORS OR EDITORS Give in inverted form the names of *all* the authors in the order listed on the title page, inserting an ampersand (&) just before the last author.

Gemmill, E., & Mayhew, N. (1995). *Changing values in medieval Scotland: A study of prices, money, and weights and measures.* Cambridge: Cambridge University Press.

REVISED EDITION OF A BOOK Abbreviate the edition ("2nd," "Rev.," "Enl.") as indicated on its title page.

Ornstein, R. E. (1977). *The psychology of consciousness* (2nd ed.). New York: Harcourt.

BOOK WITH A CORPORATE AUTHOR Alphabetize corporate authors by the first significant word of the name. When the author and publisher are the same, use "Author" where the publisher's name would appear.

American Psychological Association. (1995). *Publication manual of the American Psychological Association* (4th ed.). Washington, DC: Author.

BOOK WITH NO AUTHOR Alphabetize under the first significant word in the title. Thus, in the following example, the entry would be alphabetized under "Nineteen."

> *The 1995 NEA almanac of higher education.* (1995). Washington DC: National Education Association.

BOOK WITH TWO OR MORE VOLUMES

> Eisenstein, E. L. (1979). *The printing press as an agent of change* (Vols. 1–2). New York: Cambridge University Press.

BOOK IN TRANSLATION

> Turgenev, I. (1965). *Fathers and sons* (R. Edmonds, Trans.). New York: Penguin. (Original work published 1861)

GOVERNMENT DOCUMENT

> National Institute of Mental Health. (1982). *Television and behavior: Ten years of scientific progress and implications for the eighties* (DHHS Publication No. ADM 82-1195). Washington, DC: U.S. Government Printing Office.

ARTICLE IN A ONE-AUTHOR COLLECTION

> Orwell, G. (1956). Why I write. In *The Orwell reader: Fiction, essays, and reportage by George Orwell* (pp. 390–396). New York: Harcourt.

ARTICLE/CHAPTER IN AN EDITED COLLECTION

> Walhstrom, B. (1994). Communication and technology: Defining a feminist presence in research and practice. In C. Selfe & S. Hilligoss (Eds.), *Literacy and computers: The complications of teaching and learning with technology* (pp. 171–185). New York: MLA.

ARTICLE/CHAPTER IN A REFERENCE WORK

> Frye, N., Baker, S., & Perkins, G. (1985). Classicism. In *The Harper handbook to literature* (p. 105). New York: Harper.

11d "References" Entries: Articles

The main divisions for each entry of an article in a periodical are as follows:

1. **Author** Give the author's last name first, then the initials. If there is more than one author, list them all, and insert an ampersand (&) before the last author.
2. **Date of Publication** Place the year of publication within parentheses. If you are citing a daily, weekly, or monthly periodical, include the month and, if applicable, the day within the parentheses after the year.
3. **Article** State the article's full title, capitalizing only the first word of the title and subtitle as well as all proper nouns. Do not italicize (underline) the full title or use quotation marks around it.
4. **Publication Information** This part of the entry should include the *name of the periodical* in italics (underlined), the *volume number* in italics (underlined), and the *page references*, using "pp." only before newspaper citations.

The following are variations and/or examples of APA bibliographic style for citing articles in periodicals.

ARTICLE IN AN ACADEMIC JOURNAL

> Harris, M. (1989). Composing behaviors of one- and multi-draft writers. *College English, 51*, 174–191.

If each issue is paginated separately, include the issue number in parentheses immediately after the volume number, leaving no space between the two elements. Do not italicize (underline) the issue number.

> *Journal of Social Issues, 37*(2), 1–7.

ARTICLE/CHAPTER IN AN ANNUAL Treat annuals with regular publication dates as periodicals, not books.

> Kessler, R. C., Price, R. H., & Wortman, C. B. (1985). Social factors in psychotherapy: Stress, social support, and coping processes. *Annual Review of Psychology, 36*, 531–572.

Roberts, S. K. (1981, September). Artificial intelligence. *Byte, 63*, 164–178.

China: Kind words, little effect. (1995, August 7). [Editorial]. *The New York Times*, p. A12.

11e "References" Entries: Other Sources

Couture, B. (1993). Against relativism: Restoring truth in writing. *Journal of Advanced Composition, 13*(1), 111–134. (ERIC Document Reproduction Service No. EJ 455 641)

Benton, R. (Director). (1984). *Places in the heart* [Film]. Los Angeles: Tri-Star.

ELECTRONIC SOURCES   Full citations in the "References" section contain the author, the date of publication, the title of the source, and the name of the periodical or work. This information is followed by type of electronic source (online, CD-ROM), the volume numbers, and the appropriate page or paragraph numbers. If the information is available on the Internet, provide the address. The statement of availability is a substitute for the name of the publisher, typically provided for print references, and is provided to aid the reader in locating the information.

Internet Listserv

Saunderg. (1994). September 24. Re: Origin(s) of race. ANTHRO-L (Anthropology Listserv) [Online]. Available E-mail: anthro-l@bvm.Bitnet

Online service

Rubin, A. M. (1995, July 28). Using pop culture to combat teen violence [19 paragraphs]. *Chronicle of Higher Education. Academe This Week*. [Online service]. Available gopher or http://chronicle.merit.edu

Online journal article

Lindsay, R. K. (1991, January 8). Electronic journals of proposed research [30 paragraphs]. *EJournal* [Online serial], 1(1). Available E-mail: tjennings@suny.edu

Basic
Document
Design

12 Document and Page Design

For years, guides like this one offered only the briefest advice about the appearance of college papers. Most notable were instructions to students to use standard 8½ × 11-inch paper, to leave 1-inch margins on all four sides, to double-space between lines, and to clean their typewriter keys before typing their paper. The assumption was that, if this writing were ever to be published, someone else (not the writer, but a designer or compositor) would be responsible for how that writing looked on the printed page. Meanwhile, the few things that student writers had to do—like putting their name and page number at the top right of each page, starting with page two, or setting a new, temporary left margin—they did manually.

With word processing, all this changes. Writers can control not only the words on the page, but also the appearance of those words. While the goal of producing a neat, legible text remains, even the most basic commands about name and page numbering or new margins now have to be entered as software instructions. Your name and the page number, for example, have to be entered as what is called a running header. Meanwhile, nearly all programs give you the tools to control many other aspects of how your printed paper will look—especially when used in conjunction with a laser printer. While few teachers may expect you to master all the features necessary to produce professional-looking documents, you should understand the fundamentals of document design, including the basics of margin settings and fonts, that determine the appearance of any printed text. The more you learn how to change the settings on your word processor, the more control you have over how your writing looks to readers.

12a Word Processing Default Settings

Although laser printers and sophisticated word processors give you considerable control over the appearance of your documents, in most cases you can produce acceptable documents using the default settings on your word processor. Programs generally assume

- standard 8½ × 11-inch paper in portrait (long), as compared to landscape (wide), page orientation
- no multiple columns
- printing on one side of the paper only
- a minimum 1-inch margin on all four sides

Even with these default settings, you will still need to control formatting options in three areas:

- headers and page numbering
- paragraph margins
- font and typefaces

12b Headers, Title Pages, Page Numbering

With all college essays, you are required to supply certain information before the start of the paper itself: your name, the course name and number, your teacher's name, the due date of the assignment, and the title of your work. The simple way to present this information is in a heading on your first page of text, as in the section immediately following.

HEADING ON FIRST PAGE

Peter Larson
English 101-023
Ms. Hermann
18 September 1995

The Necessity of Change

Thomas Carlyle wrote, "Change, indeed, is painful; yet ever needful" (930). His statement is true not only about life, but also about literature. Change is an integral part of many literary works. British literature is full of works about life and change. James Joyce's "The Dead" is a short story about a man whose life is changing on several levels. "The Daughters of the Late Colonel" by Katherine Mansfield is also a story about changes; however, it is the story of two women who lose their father. Though the stories differ in style, content, and character, the underlying theme of change is present in both.

Always check with your instructor to see if other information is needed or if you are required to use a separate title page (see the next section).

TITLE PAGE There is no one way to prepare a title page, so check with your instructor to see if there are specific course or school guidelines. As a general rule, a title page will contain the title at the top or center of the page, followed by the same information as in the section above—all centered. Computer-generated **headers** (information that appears at the top of every page) and **footers** (information that appears at the bottom of every page) should not be included on your title page, nor should any page numbers. The first page of text, not the title page, should count as page one once page numbering begins. Finally, you would normally repeat your title on that first page, centered at the top.

The Necessity of Change

Peter Larson
English 101-023
Ms. Hermann
18 September 1995

HEADERS AND HEADINGS Do not confuse your **heading**, which contains information about your paper and appears once at the top of page 1 when you are not using a separate title page, with your header, which contains your last name and the current page number, and needs to appear at the top of every printed page, starting with page 2.

Larson 2

    is not only directed at his party companions, but also at his countrymen in general. Miss Ivors is the first to bring this fact to his attention. She is an avid supporter of the Irish cause, as her clothing attests: "The large brooch which was fixed on her collar bore an Irish device" (2015).

A header in a college essay should contain

- your last name
- a space
- the command for inserting the current page number

Each word processing program provides a means by which you can automatically insert information, such as a header, on every page. You should learn how to do this, rather than inserting the header manually on every page.

PAGE NUMBERING WITHOUT A TITLE PAGE   Since your heading already appears on page one, format your document so that the page numbering begins with "2" on the second page.

PAGE NUMBERING WITH A TITLE PAGE   When you have a separate title page, format your document to skip two pages (the title page and page one) before starting to print the header. Make sure that the page numbering starts with "2."

OTHER PAGE-NUMBERING OPTIONS   Certain disciplines may require the use of additional numbering systems in formal research papers—for example, the use of lower-case Roman numerals for introductory material or Arabic numerals placed as footers on the first page of every new chapter.

12c Paragraph Margins

There are two important things to note about word processing paragraphs.

First, a paragraph in word processing is purely a technical entity consisting of all text between **end-of-paragraph markers**—the space or character you create each time you press ENTER in most word processing programs. Thus, a "Works Cited" entry is technically one paragraph—as is your name, the date, and other information at the top of page one—simply because you have pressed ENTER to move to the next line.

Second, a paragraph normally has two different left margins: one setting for the first line (the line immediately below the last end-of-paragraph marker) and another setting for all subsequent lines of text. The first line of text is sometimes called the **paragraph margin**, as compared to the normal **left margin** for all subsequent lines of text.

LEFT MARGINS AND EXTENDED QUOTATIONS   All word processing programs allow you to reset the left margins temporarily, another function you should master. There are at least two places where you will need to change the left paragraph margins in a college essay: in extended quotations, where the left margin is moved in one inch; and in the "Works Cited" section of your paper (if you are following MLA style), which uses a **hanging margin** or **hanging indent**, in which the first line of each citation is flush left and all subsequent lines are indented.

You also need one-inch indented left margin whenever you are quoting three or more lines of poetry. Remember to retain the poem's own indentions and different margin settings.

The relationship between the paragraph margin and the regular left margin results in the following different types, or shapes, of paragraphs:

Indented paragraph

> The confrontation with Miss Ivors is not the only one that causes a change in Gabriel Conroy. After the party, he and Gretta retire to their hotel room. Gabriel is filled with desire for his wife, but he is disappointed when they arrive at the room. Gretta has no thoughts of making love to her husband. . . .
>
> In "The Daughters of the Late Colonel," Katherine Mansfield presents a story of two girls who are faced with great change after the death of their father. . . .

Block paragraph

> Please consider my application for the part-time intern position in your new community outreach program. I am both trained and ready to do such work.
>
> As part of a social work course I am taking this term, I have served seventy-five hours as a volunteer at the Reich Senior Citizens Center. . . .

Hanging paragraph

> Bolter, J. David. *Turing's Man: Western Culture in the Computer Age*. Chapel Hill: U of North Carolina P, 1984.
>
> Brand, Stewart. *The Media Lab: Inventing the Future at MIT*. New York: Viking, 1987.

For most college essays, use indented paragraphs either by setting your word processor appropriately or by using the block-paragraph format and the tab key at the start of each paragraph.

(Note that the block format is normally used in personal letters, where the text is single-spaced and a blank line is inserted between paragraphs.)

RIGHT MARGINS Professional setting usually entails an aligned, or **justified** right margin. For college essays, however, most readers prefer the normal fixed spacing between words that results in an unjustified, or **ragged**, right margin.

12d Fonts and Typefaces

In the past, writers often made just one decision about typefaces: whether to get a typewriter with **pica** (large—ten characters per inch) type or **elite** (small—twelve characters per inch) type. Today, with computer-generated type at your disposal, you have many more options, although you may choose to ignore these options and work with the default type in your word processor. To take advantage of the different fonts and type styles available to you, however, you need to understand three things.

PROPORTIONAL AND FIXED FONTS Typewriters and many computer programs work largely with **fixed fonts**—that is, each letter, regardless of its actual width, occupies the same space so that a narrow letter such as *I* takes up as much space as a wide letter such as *M*. With **proportional fonts**, narrow letters take up less space than wide letters so that the eight-letter word *Illinois* looks narrower than the seven-letter word *Wyoming*.

FIXED FONT	PROPORTIONAL FONT
Illinois	Illinois
Wyoming	Wyoming

The advantages of proportional fonts:

- They can be easy to read in printed form.
- They give a professional-looking appearance.

One of the advantages of laser printers and new, high-powered word processing programs is the ease with which they allow writers to work with proportional fonts and, thus, to produce professional-looking documents. Proportional fonts are, however, often more difficult to read on the screen. They are also a problem when a writer wants to list items in columns; because each letter takes up a slightly different amount of space, columns don't line up exactly. If you use proportional fonts, use the tab key rather than the space bar to align columns.

The bottom line is that proportional fonts are considered more attractive and seem to be the wave of the future whether or not they offer immediate advantages to writers and readers who are principally concerned with content.

FONT SIZE　Fonts are measured in **points**, with 72 points to an inch. College documents are traditionally prepared using 12-point fonts (the size of pica type), while the smaller 10-point fonts (the size of elite type) are usually preferred for personal correspondence or where it may be important to fit more text on a single page. For most academic writing, use large or **boldface** fonts sparingly, and then mainly for titles or for subtitles within papers (as in the multiple headings used in scientific documents), since they can overwhelm a document.

FONT STYLES (OR TYPEFACE)　The characteristics of a particular set of letters and numbers—its design—have traditionally been called a **typeface**; the term **font** refers to all the letters, numbers, punctuation marks, and so forth of that typeface in a particular size. (Increasingly, this distinction is being lost, the word *font* being used for both size and design.)

One difference among fonts involves the presence or absence of **serifs**—cross strokes at the ends of the main strokes of many letters (for example, M). While traditional typefaces like Times Roman have serifs, the more modern, cleaner-looking typefaces like Univers do not and are referred to as **sans serif** type (for example, M). Most fonts are proportional, with Times Roman and Univers being among the most common; the two most common fixed fonts are Courier and Elite.

Times Roman (serif): Alabama, Arkansas
Univers (sans serif): Maryland, Vermont
```
Courier (serif): Wisconsin,
  Michigan
```
Elite (serif): Oregon, Arizona

Serif type is more popular when you are dealing with body text; sans serif type works well for headings and large-font titles. Try to establish some logic and consistency in your use of typefaces, introducing new ones sparingly and only as needed.

12e Other Design Features

Word processing programs increasingly permit users to integrate pictures directly into their text, often allowing the text to wrap around the picture. Whether you take advantage of this feature or not, be sure to number all illustrations sequentially (Illustration 1, Illustration 2, and so forth) and to supply a brief caption for each, using the illustration number in your text to refer to the actual illustration.

The use of varied fonts and graphics along with the ability to lay out and print text in multiple columns allows users to produce attractive, even professional-looking, newsletters as well as many other nonacademic documents. Unquestionably, this increased access to such software will encourage the production of a wide variety of documents in future college writing, and writing guides such as this one will have extensive sections on such matters. The following sections, however, deal only with a few miscellaneous matters related to the formatting of traditional essays.

FORCED PAGE BREAK   All word processing programs have a command to end the current page and start a new one—for example, at the end of a separate title page. Some programs also have a special command, called a **conditional page break**, that only breaks a page when there is a limited amount of space left at the start of a new paragraph. Either form of page break allows you to keep important information together on a single page.

HARD SPACES   Word processing programs are always looking for places to break lines within a paragraph and normally use the spaces between the word to do so. With many words, or with phrases like "Los Angeles" or "Dr. Jones," or between ellipses, however, a line break between the first and subsequent parts is disruptive. Inserting a **hard space** instead of simply using the spacebar tells the program not to allow a line break at that particular point; the hard space binds itself to the next character.

HYPHENS: REGULAR, SOFT, HARD   Word processing calls for three kinds of hyphens, all of which look the same when printed but must be entered differently in the editing stage.

- **Regular hyphen:** used to allow the program to decide when to break a hyphenated word (like *self-important*) at the end of a line
- **Soft hyphen:** used to break a word at the end of a line (called *soft* since it disappears if the format of the document changes and the word is no longer divided between two lines)
- **Hard hyphen:** used to keep a two-part, hyphenated term (like the phone number 500-1286) from breaking at the end of a line (called *hard* since it bonds itself to the next character)

DASH   Although a dash is normally formed by using two hyphens, many word processing programs will allow a line to break between two regular hyphens. To avoid this, you must create the dash from a hard hyphen followed by a regular hyphen. (The regular hyphen at the end allows the line to break after the dash.)

As an alternative, you may wish to check your word processing program for a special character called an **em dash**, which is a full-length solid dash, and use that in your document.

TABS   To shift a fixed distance left or right or to move any line, you must use the tab settings of your word processing program, not the spacebar. This is especially true if you are using a proportional font and, thus, the spacebar has no fixed value. Becoming comfortable with setting and moving tabs takes time and practice. So find this feature on your word processing program, and begin to use it.

C H E C K L I S T 10

Document Design

For a standard college essay, make certain you have

- included a one-inch margin on all four sides
- double-spaced all text
- used a clear, readable 10- to 12-point font
- incorporated your name and page number as a header on every page starting with page 2
- indented extended quotations one inch in from the left margin
- started your "Works Cited" on a new page
- fixed all awkward line breaks involving dashes or ellipses by using hard characters (that is, hard hyphens, hard spaces, and so forth)

Creating a Cover Letter

Block format for business correspondence is simple and straightforward; it typically uses single spacing within paragraphs and double spacing between them. Because of the added space introduced between paragraphs, it is possible to use a smaller (10 point) font in this format, which often allows you to keep your correspondence to a single page.

1219 West Eagle Street
Linden, AL 35678
November 12, 1995

James H. Gregory, Director of Personnel Services
Veterans Administration Hospital
19 Rocky Hill Road
Tuscaloosa, AL 35412

Dear Mr. Gregory:

Please consider my application for the part-time intern position in your new community outreach program. I am both trained and ready to do such work.

As part of a social work course I am taking this term, I have served seventy-five hours as a volunteer at the Reich Senior Citizens Center. This spring I will only be taking two courses, both related to my senior project in community mental health services.

I have enclosed my vita, which has my address and phone number as well as information about obtaining letters of reference.

Sincerely yours,

Linda Forbes

enclosure

Note: Leave three lines' space between the complimentary close and the correspondent's name for the signature.

Designing a Résumé

The two parts of a résumé are fairly simple and straightforward: centered individual lines that include name, address, and telephone number; individual lines that feature a category (like "Education") at the left margin, followed by two tab stops—for example, one at 2.5 inches and the other at 3.5 inches—the first for the years and the second for a description or explanation. *Note:* You may have to adjust your tab settings to get the right spacing. Below is a sample.

Linda Forbes
1219 West Eagle Street
Linden, AL 35678
205-752-0871

| Education | 1992 | University of Alabama, B.A. |
| Experience | 1991 | Organized and charted records for University Health Service. Served as a community volunteer for local United Way agency. |

When the explanatory text runs over to two or more lines, switch to a hanging-paragraph format for the body of the résumé, perhaps with the paragraph margin at 1 inch and the left margin at 3 inches. Then set the first tab stop to 3 inches as well.

Sentences
and Words

Effective writing contains carefully structured sentences made up of well-chosen and well-arranged words. Some writers prefer to pay attention to these elements at the end of the writing process, when they are pleased with the content and organization of the project.

To check sentence structure, move your cursor sentence by sentence through your text. As you analyze each sentence, you may also decide to examine word choice. With an online thesaurus, you can get instant suggestions on alternative word choices. Use the thesaurus sparingly, though. You want to sound like yourself, not someone else. As a rule, substitute only words that are part of your working vocabulary and that fit the context of your sentence.

13 Effective Sentences

This section offers advice on active and passive voice, parallel construction, choppy sentences, and wordiness. Effective sentence structure and word choice can help you improve the overall style of your sentences and communicate your meaning clearly.

13a Active and Passive Voice

In the **active voice**, the subject acts; in the **passive voice**, the subject is acted upon. Use active verbs unless you have a reason to do otherwise. Reserve the passive for specific purposes: to de-emphasize the agent or doer of the action or to create greater coherence between sentences.

ACTIVE VOICE   Where possible, use the active voice with subjects acting on objects.

> ➤ The teacher played the piano.

The subject of the sentence, "teacher," is active. The teacher is responsible for the action of playing the piano.

PASSIVE VOICE   Passive verbs are constructed by combining a form of *to be* and the past-participle form of the verb. When converting a sentence from passive to active, ask yourself who or what acted, and then use your answer as the subject of the sentence.

> ~~It was~~ voted ~~by the~~ jury to acquit the defendant.
> ^{The} ^{voted}

To determine how to transform this sentence, ask, "Who voted to acquit the defendant?" Your answer produces the active sentence "The jury voted to acquit the defendant."

Sometimes you may *choose* to use the passive voice. You may want to draw attention to or away from the subject.

> John was struck by a passing car.

The writer wants to focus on John in this sentence. The passive is effective here.

ACTIVE   The police officer caught the thief.

PASSIVE   The thief was caught by the police officer.

If the writer wants to emphasize the police officer, the active voice is best. But if the writer wants to emphasize the thief, the passive voice is more effective.

> Millions died in the Auschwitz concentration camp. They were remembered by survivors during a recent memorial service.

The first sentence in the above example focuses on "millions" who died and is in the active voice. The second sentence, which is in the passive voice, begins with "they"—a pronoun reference to the "millions"—and links the second sentence with the first.

13b Parallel Construction

Use parallel construction to show the relationships among similar ideas. In the following sentences, the balance of elements heightens the effect of the ideas being conveyed.

> Do not ask what your country can do for you. Ask what you can do for your country.

> A nation of the people, for the people, and by the people shall not perish from the earth.

Use Parallel Sentence Structure

- Use repetition effectively.

  ➤ Give me liberty or give me death.

- Make sure all items in a series are presented in the same grammatical form.

  ➤ People select foreign cars for their value, ~~because they~~
     their performance,
  ~~perform well,~~ and their style.

- Use coordinating conjunctions (*and, but, for, nor, or, so, yet*) to link and balance similar concepts.

  ➤ The federal government is giving more power to states and local municipalities *and* lowering income taxes.

- Use correlative conjunctions (*either . . . or; neither . . . nor; not only . . . but also*) to link clauses.

  ➤ *Either* stay *or* go away.

13c Coordination and Subordination

Coordination refers to the use of **coordinate conjunctions** (*and, but, for, nor, or, so, yet*) to link parts of sentences.

Subordination refers to placing ideas of lesser importance in subordinate (dependent) clauses and placing more important ideas in the main clause. Using the appropriate **subordinating conjunctions**—the words that connect the ideas—helps readers understand how different ideas relate to one another. Subordinating conjunctions such as the following are used in subordination: *after, although, as, as if, as though, because, before, even though, if, since, so that, than, that, though, unless, until, when, where, whereas, while.*

Although subordination can strengthen your writing, excessive subordination can ruin it. If your sentences go on and on, try shortening them by combining sentences or by deleting unnecessary uses of *that* and *which.*

Use subordinate clauses carefully, making sure that you express ideas or concepts appropriately.

➤ They stopped for lunch and spent time talking.

In the above example, the clauses express concepts that match; therefore, coordination is effective. In the example below, the clauses in the unrevised sentence do not appear to match. The subordinate conjunction *after* gives the reader an indication of the relationship between the clauses in this sentence.

> They went shopping and they talked about the current state of affairs in government.

REVISED After they went shopping, they talked about the current state of affairs in government.

Use Coordination and Subordination Effectively

- Combine equally important short sentences by cutting unnecessary words and by adding needed words and appropriate coordinating conjunctions.

  > Passengers can visit the island at their leisure. If they want, they can remain on board.

  REVISED Passengers can either visit the island at their leisure or remain on board.

- Reduce less important sentences to phrases or dependent clauses, and combine them with the main clause by using subordinating conjunctions.

  > I worked on the project all night long. But I knew our group would fail.

  REVISED I worked on the project all night long even though I knew our group would fail.

- Remove unnecessary, repetitive words between sentences.

  > Beekeepers use a centrifuge. The centrifuge is used to extract honey that comes from a comb.

  REVISED Beekeepers use centrifuges to extract honey that comes from combs.

- Reduce less important sentences or clauses to phrases, using *-ing* or *-ed* words at the beginning or end of a sentence.

  > She has become bored by routine tax-law work. She hopes to become a defense attorney.

  REVISED Bored by routine tax law, she hopes to become a defense attorney.

CHECKLIST 12

If your writing has many short, choppy sentences, you may need to combine some of those sentences, using either coordination or subordination.

➤ Computers can do some amazing things. ~~They can~~ play *such as,*

  chess. ~~They can~~ write music. *and* ~~They can~~ draw pictures.

➤ Richard Gregory is my former boss. ~~He~~ has a short temper.

13d Wordy Sentences

Wordy sentences can obscure your meaning. Aim for clear, direct sentence structure so readers can follow your ideas.

1. Substitute **appositives** (words that mean the same thing as the word to which they refer) for clauses beginning with *who* or *which.*

   ➤ Mr. Stevens, ~~who was~~ my former neighbor, won his

     lawsuit.

2. Delete **expletives** (words such as *it is, here is,* and *there is* that are added to a sentence without adding to the meaning of the sentence).

   ➤ ~~There was~~ a teacher in my school ~~who~~ never took *A*

     roll.

3. Use **compound modifiers** (modifiers made up of more than one word) instead of prepositional and verbal phrases.

   ➤ They built the house out of lumber ~~dried in a kiln.~~ *kiln-dried*

Replace Wordy Expressions with One-Word Substitutes

INSTEAD OF	USE
at this point in time	now
because of the fact that	because
be of the opinion that	think
during the same time that	when
has the ability	can
in spite of the fact that	although
in today's world	today
red in color	red
until such time as	until

4. Eliminate unnecessary words, choosing simple one-word expressions rather than longer phrases (see Checklist 13).

➤ The company is taking applications ~~at this point in time~~. *now.*

14 Errors in Sentence Wording

14a Misplaced Modifiers

Modifiers are words, phrases, or clauses that describe the words around them. Modifiers are **misplaced** if readers are unable to determine what the modifiers describe or explain. To correct a sentence with a misplaced modifier, either move the modifier to a new position or rewrite the sentence.

➤ Marching across the field, the fight song ~~rang out~~ for all to hear. *the band played*

It is the band, not the fight song, that is doing the marching.

➤ To be successful in business, ~~ambition is essential~~. *a person must be ambitious.*

Placing the word "ambition" next to "business" implies that ambition, not a person, can be successful.

➤ Joe found a twenty-dollar bill ~~walking home~~. *While walking home*

Joe, not the twenty-dollar bill, was walking home.

MISPLACED LIMITING MODIFIERS **Limiting modifiers** are words that restrict or limit the meaning of the word or word group they modify. Place limiting modifiers *almost*, *even*, *exactly*, *hardly*, *just*, *merely*, *nearly*, *only*, *scarcely*, and *simply* in front of the word or words you want to modify.

➤ We must *only* go as far as the next town.

The writer is saying that going to the next town is all that we've got to do. The focus is on what has to be done—only going as far as the next town.

➤ We must go *only* as far as the next town.

The writer is focusing on how far we have to go—only to the next town.

➤ The instructor did not *even* call me once.

The writer is focusing on the fact that the instructor not only didn't do other things, he/she didn't even call her.

➤ The instructor did not call me *even* once.

The writer focuses only on the act of calling, noting that the instructor didn't do it even one time.

SQUINTING MODIFIERS   A modifier that could refer to the preceding or following words is said to **squint**. Be sure to place modifiers where the reference is clear. Try moving phrases around so your meaning is unambiguous.

➤ ~~He said before noon~~ he'd be here.
[handwritten: Before noon, he]

or

➤ He said before noon ~~he'd be here~~.
[handwritten: he'd be here]

In the unrevised sentence above, ''before noon'' could refer to either ''he said'' or ''he'd be here.''

DANGLING MODIFIERS   Modifiers are said to be **dangling** when they fail to modify logically any word or words in a sentence. To correct a dangling modifier, ask who or what is responsible for the action described in the opening word group. Immediately after the *-ing* word group, name that person or thing.

➤ Before going on vacation, the bills ~~need to be paid~~.
[handwritten: I need to pay]

➤ After cutting the grass, the garden ~~was weeded~~.
[handwritten: I weeded]

or

➤ After cutting the grass, the garden ~~was weeded~~.
[handwritten: I weeded]

➤ Studying too hard, college ~~soon became a burden~~.
[handwritten: he soon tired of his courses.]

Correcting the dangling-modifier error sometimes requires rewriting the sentence.

14b   Split Infinitives

An **infinitive** consists of *to* and a verb or verb phrase—for example, *to write, to swim well, to act quickly*. An infinitive is said to be **split** when a word or words appear between its two parts, as in *to gladly serve*. Infinitives can be split in informal writing,

but in college writing and other more formal situations, reword
sentences that contain split infinitives.

> After work, he likes to ~~briskly~~ run *briskly* along the riverbank.

"Briskly" modifies the infinitive "to run."

14c Shifts in Construction

Some sentence problems seem accidental and are thus hard to
label. This section covers errors that result when a writer in-
advertently makes any shift: a shift away from topics in the
subject of the sentence; a shift in tense; a shift in pronoun person and number; and a shift from statements to commands or
from statements to wishes, often called shifts in mood.

SHIFT FROM SUBJECT TO PREDICATE   When you start an idea
in the subject part of a sentence, you must complete that idea—
not another idea—in the predicate. To correct sentences that
end up differently from the way they started, you may need to
reconsider completely the point you want to make.

> ~~When I bake~~ *Baking* cookies relaxes me.

    or

> When I bake cookies *, I relax.* ~~relaxes me.~~

In the first revision, the subject matches the predicate. In the
second revision, the predicate completes the sentence structure
implied by the subject.

> ~~My promotion~~ *I was promoted* to manager ~~was the position I wanted.~~

SHIFT IN TENSE   The verb tense used in a sentence should give
readers a clear idea of the *time* of the action described. Be consistent in using verb tense, shifting tenses only as required. An
abrupt shift in tense can confuse readers.

> Workers who ~~were~~ *are* consulted regularly feel more committed to
> the company and ~~had~~ *have* a lower rate of absenteeism.

    or

> Workers who ~~were~~ *have been* consulted regularly feel *now* more committed to
> the company and ~~had~~ *have* a lower rate of absenteeism.

The original sentence refers to an action in the past ("workers were consulted"), then switches to the present ("regularly feel"), then moves back to the past "had a lower rate"). To revise a sentence with faulty predication, you must clarify the writer's intent.

As a rule, use the present tense when referring to the actions of literary characters.

> ➤ Hamlet ~~delayed~~ *delays* because he ~~was~~ *is* overwhelmed by the events of
>
> the past few days.

SHIFT IN PRONOUN PERSON AND NUMBER   Pronoun references should be consistent throughout a paper. If you are writing about yourself, then maintain an *I* point of view throughout the paper. If you are writing directions, maintain a *you* point of view. If you start writing a paper in the third person (using pronouns such as *he, she, it,* or *they* and synonyms such as *a person, a platypus, students,* and *tourists*), a shift to *I* may be appropriate, but not a shift to *you.*

Although many teachers now recognize that *I* and *you* are used in many writing situations, including some academic publications, some teachers still oppose the use of *I* or *you* in college papers. Remember that it is possible, and often better, to state your opinions without using *I.* If you are uncertain about using *I* or *you,* check with your instructor.

> ➤ Students often wonder why they don't learn how to speak a
>
> foreign language fluently. ~~If you~~ *Individuals who* want to learn how to speak a
>
> foreign language , ~~you~~ should live in that country.

> ➤ The policy stated that since we had completed the assignment
>
> already, ~~you~~ *we* did not have to stay.

> *or*

> ➤ The policy stated that ~~since we~~ *anyone who* had completed the assignment
>
> already , ~~you~~ did not have to stay.

SHIFT IN MOOD   A shift in mood refers to a shift in the approach to a topic. In the **indicative mood,** ideas are expressed in a matter-of-fact way.

> ➤ Your room needs to be cleaned.

The **imperative mood** is characterized by commands or requests.

➤ Clean your room.

The **subjunctive mood** refers to wishes or statements contrary to fact.

➤ If I were going to clean my room, I would have done it already.

Avoid abrupt shifts from statements to commands. If a shift is necessary, signal the change to your readers.

➤ Next, I will explain how to format a disk. First, insert the disk into the disk drive.

The writer of the above sentences prepares readers for a shift in the way the topic will be approached.

➤ The directions suggest first laying out and identifying all the parts. *The next step is to apply* ~~Next, apply~~ the first coat.

Since the writer intends to explain the steps in painting, not to give *direct commands*, the writer has shifted from the imperative to the indicative mood.

SHIFT FROM DIRECT TO INDIRECT DISCOURSE **Direct discourse** consists of the actual words of a speaker, with quotation marks around the words. **Indirect discourse** is a translation or restatement of what the speaker said; no quotation marks are used unless a portion of the original words are included in the restatement. Indirect discourse usually begins with something like "He said that . . ." and is followed by a restatement of the speaker's words.

DIRECT DISCOURSE   The news commentator said, "The hearing has ended for today but will resume tomorrow."

INDIRECT DISCOURSE   The news commentator said that the hearing had ended for today but would resume tomorrow.

or

➤ The news commentator said that the hearing had "ended for today but will resume tomorrow."

15 Errors in Punctuating Sentences

Sentences begin with a capital letter and end with an end punctuation mark, most often a period. Students frequently have difficulty punctuating sentences—using end punctuation when there is no complete sentence (creating a fragment) or punctuating two or more complete sentences as if they were a single sentence (run-on sentence or comma splice).

15a Fragments

A **sentence** is a group of words that contains a subject and a **finite verb** (a verb with tense) and that expresses a complete thought. A **sentence fragment** is a group of words that is punctuated like a sentence (that is, it begins with a capital letter and ends with end punctuation) but lacks one or more of the elements of a sentence. Although on occasion you might use a fragment intentionally for stylistic effect, it is best to avoid fragments in academic writing.

> Although he is a successful businessman. *he wants to become a teacher.*

Be careful not to mistake "although" for "however." "However, he is a successful businessman" would be a complete sentence.

> ~~Whatever~~ you think. *I'll do whatever ___ is right.*

In casual conversation, "Whatever you think" is acceptable. It is not acceptable, however, in academic writing.

Add Needed Words to Fragments

- Supply the missing subject.

  > ~~Went~~ downtown. *She went*

- Supply the missing subject and the correct finite verb.

  > ~~Having~~ known her for twenty years. *I have*

- Attach the fragment to an independent clause.

  > Although she wants to go to college.

  REVISED   Although she wants to go to college, she plans to work for a year before she enrolls.

15b Comma Splices

A **comma splice** occurs when independent clauses are joined with a comma rather than with a semicolon or a conjunction (and another clause), or severed with a period.

> The acting was competent, the direction was faulty.

Repair Comma Splices

- Join the independent parts on both sides of the comma splice with a semicolon.

  ➤ He works all day﹐ he plays volleyball all evening.

- Show a clearer relationship between the two independent clauses by using a subordinating conjunction to connect them, thus turning one of them into a dependent clause.

  ➤ Because he works all day, he enjoys those evenings when he plays volleyball.

- End the first sentence with a period. Make the second sentence into a freestanding one.

  ➤ He works all day﹐ *He* he plays volleyball all evening.

C H E C K L I S T 15

15c Run-On Sentences

Run-on (or **fused**) **sentences** are aptly labeled. They run on and on with neither the necessary punctuation to separate them nor the appropriate conjunctions to join them. Sometimes writers create run-on sentences accidentally because they want to link closely related ideas.

➤ I sang softly *but* it still scared the dog.

Separate Run-On Sentences

- Join independent clauses with appropriate conjunctions.
- Separate independent clauses with semicolons.
- Revise independent clauses by making them into separate sentences.

  ➤ What a summer we did just about everything a child would want to do we went camping, we went to the beach, and we went boating.

  REVISED   What a summer! We did just about everything a child would want to do: we went camping, we went to the beach, and we went boating.

C H E C K L I S T 16

16 Effective Word Choice

Adapting your language—your choice of words—to the audience, occasion, and purpose of your papers will help you to communicate your meaning more clearly to readers.

16a Formal and Informal Words

Different words and expressions are appropriate for different occasions. Just as you would not wear cut-offs to a wedding, you would not describe a literary figure as "the pits" in a paper; to do this would be inappropriately informal.

If you are unsure of the audience and purpose of your writing, maintain a general level of usage. If you know the audience and purpose, then adapt your usage to the context. Keep in mind, however, that words that are either too formal or too casual tend to draw attention to themselves and thus should serve some constructive purpose when used.

➤ His departure left the country paralyzed.

The word "departure" is appropriate here.

➤ If he is not reappointed to the social club, he may ~~depart~~ the
    leave

organization.

In this sentence, "depart" is too formal.

16b Specific and General Words

Specific words provide precise, sensory, or concrete details. **General words** convey inexact, intangible, and often abstract concepts. Some writing tasks require more use of abstractions

Choose Precise Words

INSTEAD OF	CONSIDER
a *good* movie	a *suspenseful, terrifying, lighthearted* movie
a *nice* smile	a *winning, angelic, purposeful* smile
someone I know	*a friend, an acquaintance, a colleague, a co-worker*
walked	*paced, strutted, strolled, marched*

than others; an essay on democracy and communism would include more abstract terms than would an autobiographical essay. As an overall rule, use the most precise word you can find for a general term, and support general or abstract statements with abundant details or specific references.

➤ The president's knowledge of *domestic issues* is superior to his understanding of *foreign policy*. He has worked harder on developing an innovative health-care policy, than on nuclear-arms issues.

"Domestic issues" and "foreign policy," abstract terms, are followed by specific references to "health care" and "nuclear arms."

16c Figurative Language

Figurative language refers to similes, metaphors, and other literary techniques. Although effective figurative language can help readers visualize your meaning, ineffective figurative language can ruin the intended effect. In general, state ideas in your own words, and avoid clichés and trite expressions that add nothing distinctive to your meaning. *Note:* A particular danger in using trite expressions is the **mixed metaphor**, a situation that occurs when a writer unknowingly allows two or more metaphoric images to clash.

➤ If you build your plans on sand, they may collapse.

REVISED   If you don't test the redesign of the menu with users, you can expect complaints.

In the revision, the specific situation is clearly implied in the sentence. In the original, it is not clear what "plans" might "collapse."

➤ We won by ~~leaps and bounds.~~ 20 points.

16d Gender-Inclusive Words

You are expected to use gender-inclusive, nonsexist words in your writing.

➤ The ~~stewardess~~ flight attendant served the first-class passengers a gourmet meal.

➤ The ~~mailman~~ carrier left the package on the front step.

➤ The department ~~chairman~~ called a meeting.

Use Gender-Inclusive Language

- Use gender-neutral terms (see section 16d): *reporter* rather than *newsman*, *to staff* rather than *to man*, *representative* rather than *congressman*.
- Use the plural to avoid the awkward use of *he* or *she* (see pages 132–133).

  ➤ A ~~writer~~ usually revises ~~his or her~~ work several times.
  (Writers ... their)

- Avoid sexist stereotyping.

  ➤ A ~~parent~~ should take good care of ~~her~~ child.
  (Parents ... their ...ren.)

  ➤ The ~~wives~~ will have an opportunity to tour the city during the conference.
  (spouses)

17 Usage Glossary

a   Use *a* before consonant sounds (*a car, a history, a union*).
an   Use *an* before vowel sounds (*an elk, an X-ray, an herb*).

accept   (verb) "to take," "to receive": *I accept the award gladly.*
except   (preposition) "not counting": *Except for the lack of plumbing, the apartment is perfect*; (verb) "to leave out": *Please except that package from the group.*

adapt   (verb) "to adjust": *Some people adapt easily to new environments.*
adept   (adjective) "skillful": *She is adept at mastering new tasks.*
adopt   (verb) "to care for as one's own": *He adopts a new image when needed.*

advice   (noun) "guidance": *My doctor gave me sound advice.*
advise   (verb) "to recommend," "to inform": *I often advise her on what to wear.*

affect   (verb) "to influence": *Technology affects people in different ways.*
effect   (noun) "consequence": *It has both positive and negative effects on job performance*; (verb) "to bring about," "to cause to occur" *Skiing effects a sense of exhilaration.*

aid (noun) "assistance": *Her role is to provide aid to homeless children*; (verb) "to assist": *She aids homeless children.*

aide (noun) "an assistant": *As an aide, she helps in countless ways.*

allude "to make reference to": *Poets frequently allude to Greek and Roman myths.*

elude "to avoid capture": *Some poems elude interpretation.*

allusion "indirect reference": *In his footnotes, Eliot explains the allusions in "The Waste Land" to readers.*

illusion "false appearance": *Her weight loss is an illusion.*

a lot (always two words) "many": *She has a lot of energy.*

alot Incorrect spelling of *a lot.*

all ready "everyone prepared": *The students are all ready to explore the Internet.*

already "previously": *Already, the teacher has assigned the first two chapters.*

all right (always two words) "satisfactory," "certainly": *It is all right to admit that you are wrong.*

alright Incorrect spelling of *all right.*

all together "everyone in one place": *When we put our resources all together, we discovered that we had more than we needed to cover our expenses.*

altogether "completely": *You have an altogether different reading list.*

altar (noun) "place of worship": *The altar was decorated with flowers.*

alter (verb) "to change": *The flowers altered the usual appearance of the church.*

among "shared by a group" (usually three or more): *They are among the ten best athletes in the school.*

between "shared by individuals" (usually two): *Tara sat between Julia and Peter.*

amount (noun) "quantity of something that cannot be counted": *The amount of money needed to fund the project is staggering*; (verb) "to equal": *It doesn't amount to much.*

number (noun) "quantity of something that can be counted":

The number of students required for state funding is 750; (verb) "to include," "to assign a number to": *The chorus numbers twenty.*

anxious "nervous, worried": *I am anxious about my grades.*
eager "characterized by enthusiastic interest": *I am eager to go on vacation.*

any more "no more": *We don't want to buy any more property.*
anymore "any longer": *We don't live here anymore.*

anyone "any person": *Did anyone come?*
any one "any member of a group": *Any one of you would be welcome.*

anyways Nonstandard for *anyway.*

anywheres Nonstandard for *anywhere.*

appraise "to calculate value": *The teacher appraises students' abilities at midterm.*
apprise "to inform": *He apprises them of their strengths and weaknesses.*

as (conjunction) "in the way that": *The computer didn't work as the instructions said it would.*
like (preposition) "similar to": *I would prefer a computer like Anna's.* Do not use *like* in place of *as* or *as if* in formal writing: *They acted as if they were drunk.*

ascent (noun) "rising," "advancement": *The ascent of the rocket into space was swift.*
assent (verb) "to agree": *I assent to the compromise*; (noun) "agreement": *After winning the school board's assent, schools began to include Darwinism in the curriculum.*

assistance (noun) "aid": *Work-study students provide assistance in the library.*
assistants (plural noun) "helpers": *The librarian always requests additional student assistants.*

bad (adjective) "not good," "sick," "sorry": *This is a bad situation.*
badly (adverb) "not well": *We have performed badly.*

bare (adjective) "naked": *I like to walk around with bare feet*; (verb) "to expose": *I bared my soul to the poetry of the moment.*

bear (noun) "animal": *The polar bear is an arctic resident*; (verb) "to carry," "to tolerate": *I cannot bear to listen to that music.*

bazaar (noun) "marketplace or fair for the sale of goods": *On our vacation to Mexico, we visited several local bazaars.*

bizarre (adjective) "strange": *It was bizarre to run into our neighbors in Mexico.*

because of See *due to/because of.*

beside (preposition) "next to": *We sat beside the president of the company.*

besides (preposition) "in addition to," "except": *Besides the members' spouses, we were the only visitors invited*; (adverb) "moreover," "also": *I don't want to go to class; besides, I love the park.*

between See *among/between.*

bring "to move an object toward something": *Bring your roommate to the party.*

take "to move an object away from something": *When you exit the train, take your belongings.*

can "to be able to do something": *With practice, you can learn the difference between* can *and* may.

may "to ask for or be granted permission": *You may not use* can *in this sentence.*

capital "city in which the seat of government is located": *Santa Fe is the capital of New Mexico*; (noun) "possessions and their value": *If we want more capital, we'll have to raise more money.*

capitol "the building that houses the legislature": *In Santa Fe, the capitol is shaped like a Zia sun symbol.*

censer (noun) "incense burner": *The censer gave off a lot of smoke.*

censor (verb) "to alter," "to delete": *Many critics would love to censor this artist's work*; (noun) "one who censors": *The censor didn't like my sentence, so he censored it.*

censure (noun) "condemnation"; (verb) "to blame," "to condemn": *The student government censured me for making that statement.*

cite (verb) "to acknowledge": *When you quote someone in a paper, be sure you cite the source.*

sight (noun) "ability to see," "something that is seen": *Wearing an eight-foot feathered headdress, he was a magnificent sight;* (verb) "to glimpse": *In Memphis last week, Elvis was sighted in the supermarket.*

site (noun) "location": *The archeological site exposed several layers of human occupation;* (verb) "to place": *We couldn't agree on where to site the gazebo.*

coarse (adjective) "rough": *The texture of the fabric is coarse.*

course (noun) "path," "unit of study": *This is a writing course.*

complement (noun) "that which completes": *The baby had the full complement of fingers and toes;* (verb) "to complete": *The printed book complements the online tutorial.*

compliment (noun) "expression of admiration": *The author paid Carol a compliment;* (verb) "to flatter": *The author complimented Carol.*

conscience (noun) "sense of right and wrong": *He reads my stories only because he has a guilty conscience.*

conscious (adjective) "aware": *He is not conscious of how others react to him.*

continual "repeatedly," "over and over": *Updating our database is a continual process.*

continuous "without interruption": *The continuous rivalry between the two of them was harmful.*

could care less Nonstandard for *couldn't care less.*

could of Nonstandard for *could have.*

council (noun) "advisory or legislative body": *The council of elders debated my future.*

counsel (noun) "advice": *Her counsel was useful;* (verb) "to give advice": *In the end, they counseled me wisely.*

criteria (plural of *criterion*) "standard for judgment": *The criteria for choosing the winner were varied.*

data (plural of *datum*) "facts": *The data are here in this research report.*

defer "to delay," "to yield": *I defer to your judgment.*

differ "to disagree," "to be unlike": *I beg to differ with you.*

deference "respect," "consideration": *We turned the music down in deference to those who wanted to sleep.*

difference "being unlike": *You and I have a difference of opinion.*

diffidence "shyness": *His diffidence accounts for his lack of a social life.*

desert (noun) "dry, barren place": *The heat of the desert was fierce*; (verb) "to leave": *I will not desert my friends.*

dessert (noun) "sweet course at the end of a meal": *Dessert is my favorite part of any meal.*

device (noun) "plan," "piece of equipment": *A mouse is a device used to move a pointer in a computer program.*

devise (verb) "to think up": *Whoever devised the mouse had a great idea.*

different from/different than *Different from* is preferred: *His attitude toward studying is different from mine.* Use *different than* when a construction using *different from* is wordy: *I am a different person than I was two years ago.*

due to "resulting from": *The bags under my eyes are due to stress.*

because of "as the result of": *My grade in the class dropped because of this assignment.*

eager See *anxious/eager.*

effect See *affect/effect.*

elude See *allude/elude.*

eminent "prominent," "important": *The professor was eminent in the field.*

immanent "operating within reality," "inherent": *Knowing which word to use is not an immanent skill—it must be learned.*

imminent "about to happen": *The test is imminent.*

enthused Use *enthusiastic*: *The grammarian was enthusiastic when he praised me for never using* enthused.

envelop (verb) "to enclose completely": *The mist will envelop us as soon as we enter the rain forest.*

envelope (noun) "wrapper, usually for a letter": *Place the invitation in the envelope.*

every one "each individual": *Every one of the athletes was tested for steroid use.*

everyone "all": *Everyone participated in the talent show.*

except See *accept/except*.

farther "at a greater distance": *Ken's rescue team traveled farther than my team did to help the victims.*
further "to a greater degree": *Ken explained that further travel was necessary to reach those in need of help.*

few, fewer "a limited number of countable items": *A few of us went to the concert.*
little, less "a small quantity of an uncountable item": *It will cost less if you make it yourself.*

formally "not casually": *The rules were formally approved by the city council.*
formerly "before": *Formerly, there were no guidelines about sorting household trash.*

good (adjective) not to be used in place of the adverb *well*: *This plan is good.*
well (adverb): *The plan will work well.*

hanged "killed by hanging": *The victors hanged their enemies.*
hung "suspended": *I hung my clothes out to dry.*

hisself Nonstandard for *himself*.

hopefully "filled with hope": *We moved hopefully toward the future.* Do not use *hopefully* to mean "I hope that," "we hope that," and so forth.

human (noun or adjective) "referring to people": *To be fallible is to be human.*
humane (adjective) "compassionate": *The humane treatment of animals is uppermost in Kate's mind.*

illusion See *allusion/illusion*.

immanent See *eminent/immanent/imminent*.
imminent See *eminent/immanent/imminent*.

imply "to suggest indirectly": *I don't mean to imply that you are wrong.*
infer "to draw a conclusion": *You may have inferred from what I said that I love you.*

incidence   "rate of occurrence": *The incidence of heart disease among Americans is high.*

incidents   "occurrences": *Many incidents during the Revolution led to American patriot losses.*

irregardless   Nonstandard for *regardless.*

its   (possessive pronoun) "belonging to it": *Its colors were iridescent.*

it's   contraction for *it is: It's a great day.*

kind of/sort of   Avoid *kind of* and *sort of* when you mean "somewhat": *The movie was somewhat scary.*

later   (adverb) "subsequently": *We'll play with the kitten later.*

latter   (adjective) "last mentioned": *Of the two stories, I prefer the latter.*

lay   (verb + object) "to place something": *He lay the book on the table.*

lie   (verb + no object) "to assume or be in a reclining position": *He went to his bedroom to lie down.*

lead   (verb) "to go before": *If you lead, we will follow;* (noun) "metal," "position at the front": *Anthony Hopkins played the lead.*

led   past participle of *lead: When you led us yesterday, we followed you.*

less   See *few/fewer/little/less.*

lessen   (verb) "to decrease": *Your bravery will lessen our fear.*

lesson   (noun) "something learned by study or experience": *That is the lesson I learned from you.*

liable   "obligated, responsible": *The landlord is liable for the roof repairs.*

likely   "future possibility": *Even if the roof isn't leaking now, it is likely to leak in the future.*

lie   See *lay/lie.*

like   See *as/like.*

little   See *few/fewer/little/less.*

loose   (adjective) "not tight": *The bolts on the car door are loose.*
lose   (verb) "to misplace," "to not win": *If we invest poorly, we might lose our money.*

many   "large number of something countable": *Many of our investments will pay off*
much   "large number of something uncountable": *Much effort was wasted in this endeavor.*

may   See *can/may.*

may be   (verb) "might be": *I may be getting better.*
maybe   (adverb) "perhaps": *Maybe we should open a savings account.*

may of   Nonstandard for *may have.*

media   Plural of *medium*: *Computers, newspapers, and TV are communications media. Media* has also come to have a singular sense in speech. Formally, use the plural.

might of   Nonstandard for *might have.*

much   See *many/much.*

must of   Nonstandard for *must have.*

nowheres   Nonstandard for *nowhere.*

number   See *amount/number.*

number of   *Number of* should be followed by a plural noun: *a number of options.*

off of   *Of* is unnecessary: *Get off the road!*

passed   (verb) past tense of *pass*: *Roaring down the road, he passed me.*
past   (adjective) "previous": *His past exploits are legendary.*

patience   (noun) "ability to wait": *Have some patience.*
patient   (adjective) "calm": *Be patient*; (noun) "someone receiving medical treatment": *I was his only patient.*

persecute   "to harass": *He felt persecuted by her attentions.*
prosecute   "to bring to trial": *She was prosecuted for grand larceny.*

personal (adjective) "relating to an individual," "private": *I don't care to share details of my personal life.*

personnel (noun) "employees": *The director of personnel takes all new employees to lunch.*

phenomena Plural of *phenomenon*, "observable facts or events": *Like other astronomical phenomena, the eclipse can be easily explained.*

plus Do not use *plus* to join independent clauses; use *moreover* or *in addition to*: *Your salary in addition to mine will cover our expenses.*

precede "to come before": *She preceded me into the house.*

proceed "to go forward," "to continue": *Please, proceed carefully into the room.*

prescribe "to order treatment": *The doctor will prescribe a medicine to relieve the pain.*

proscribe "to forbid": *Smoking is proscribed here.*

principal (noun) "chief person," "capital sum": *We may earn no interest, but we won't lose the principal*; (adjective) "most important": *The book's principal effect was to change my viewpoint on the economics of ecology.*

principle (noun) "rule," "fundamental law": *Tornadoes are based upon physical principles.*

raise (verb + object) "to lift," "to grow": *She raised her arms heavenward*; (noun) "increase in salary."

rise (verb + no object) "to get up": *Hot air balloons, however, rise more slowly*; (noun) "ascent," "hilltop": *The rise in temperature was deadly.*

respectfully "with respect": *We behave respectfully around him.*

respectively "in the order named": *We saw Kurt, Marian, and Diane, respectively, enter the building.*

right (adjective) "correct": *Roberta was the right woman for the job*; (noun) "something allowed," "location of the right side," "conservative position": *It is their right as Americans.*

rite (noun) "ceremony": *For New Yorkers, the first Yankees game is a rite of passage.*

sensual   "pleasing to the senses, especially sexual": *Don Juan was addicted to sensual experiences.*

sensuous   "pleasing to the senses, particularly with regard to the arts": *The poet's use of sensuous detail helped us see, smell, and taste the food.*

set   (verb + object) "to place something": *I set the dish on the table.*

sit   (verb + no object) "to be in or assume a sitting position": *I will sit here and eat my dinner.*

should of   Nonstandard for *should have.*

sight   See *cite/sight/site.*

site   See *cite/sight/site.*

some time   (adjective + noun) "span of time": *We have some time before the test begins.*

sometime   (adverb) "at an unspecified time": *I will probably feel nervous about it sometime soon.*

sometimes   (adverb) "now and then," "occasionally": *Sometimes I'm funny that way.*

somewheres   Nonstandard for *somewhere.*

sort of   See *kind of/sort of.*

stationary   (adjective) "not moving": *When the wind died, the sailboat was stationary.*

stationery   (noun) "letter paper": *The captain took out her stationery and wrote a letter to her husband.*

statue   "sculpture": *The* Venus de Milo *is a famous statue.*

stature   "height," "status": *The sculptor had great stature among his peers.*

statute   "law": *The town has many outdated statutes in its civil code.*

suppose to   Incorrect spelling of *supposed to.*

take   See *bring/take.*

than   (conjunction) used in comparisons: *Learning to sail was easier than learning to windsurf.*

then   (adverb) "at that time," "besides": *Then I ran the boat aground.*

that/which Use *that* for essential clauses: *The handbook that we use for English is written by Rodrigues and Tuman.* Use *which* for nonessential clauses: *The text, which was written by Rodrigues and Tuman, includes suggestions for using a word processor.*

their (pronoun) "belonging to them": *Their values are not my values.*

there (adverb) "in that place": *"The mouse is over there!" he screamed;* (expletive) used to introduce a sentence or clause: *There are some values I accept.*

they're contraction for *they are*: *They're probably more comfortable than I am.*

theirselves Nonstandard for *themselves.*

thorough (adjective) "exhaustive": *His review of my essay was thorough.*

through (preposition) "in and then out": *He did not drive through it with his car;* (adverb) "completely," "finished": *I was soaked through.*

to (preposition) "toward": *I am going to school.*

too (adverb) "in addition," "excessively": *I am going to the store, too.*

two (noun) "one more than one": *I am going to two places.*

try and Nonstandard for *try to.*

unique "one of a kind": *Among actors, Jimmy Stewart is unique.*

use to Nonstandard for *used to.*

wear (verb) "to bear or carry on the person," "to cause to degenerate by use": *You can wear what you want.*

were (verb) past tense of *be*: *You were raised to do the right thing.*

where (adverb or conjunction) "in that place": *You can go where you want.*

weather (noun) "atmosphere": *The weather outside is frightful.*

whether (conjunction) "if": *I don't know whether it will ever be delightful.*

well See *good/well.*

which See *that/which*.

which/who Do not use *which* to refer to people; use *who*: *She is the person who helped me the most.*

who/whom Use *who* for subjects and subject complements: *I will check to see who is at the door.* Use *whom* for objects: *I am the person whom she helped.*

who's Contraction of *who is*: *Who's this sweating at the table?*
whose (pronoun) possessive form of *who*: *He's the person whose tongue is burning from the chili peppers.*

would of Nonstandard for *would have*.

your (pronoun) "belonging to you": *Your cleverness amazes me.*
you're Contraction for *you are*: *You're a clever person.*

Grammar

18 Verbs

18a Subject-Verb Agreement

The subject and verb in a sentence or clause must "agree" or match. If the subject is singular, the verb must be singular; if the subject is plural, the verb must be plural. If the subject is in the first person (*I*, *we*), then the verb must be in the first person (I *am*, we *are*). The same rule holds true for subjects in the second or third person (you *are*; he/she/it *is*).

	SINGULAR	PLURAL
FIRST PERSON	I sing	we sing
	I am singing	we are singing
	I have sung	we have sung
	you sing	you sing
SECOND PERSON	you are singing	you are singing
	you have sung	you have sung
	he/she/it sings	they sing
THIRD PERSON	he/she/it is singing	they are singing
	he/she/it has sung	they have sung

INTERVENING WORDS Sometimes a word of phrase comes between the subject and the verb. Ignore that word or phrase when locating the subject and verb, making sure that the verb agrees with the subject.

> ➤ My *brother*, along with our friends, *is* looking forward to this weekend.

> ➤ One of my friends ~~are~~ ^{is} graduating.

Hint: To test subject-verb agreement, mentally recite the sentence *without* the intervening words. In other words, replace the complete subject "one of my friends is graduating" with "one is graduating."

COMPOUND SUBJECTS JOINED BY *AND* When the parts of a subject are joined by *and*, the verb is usually plural.

➤ Captain Picard and three other officers *were* honored.

➤ The coach and the quarterback *understand* what teamwork means.

The exception occurs when the subject is a single item, like a food dish (for example, strawberries and cream), formed by joining together two items.

➤ Red beans and rice *is* a popular dish in Louisiana.

Hint: To make subject-and-verb agreement easier, try substituting a pronoun for the compound subject. For instance, in the second example, above, substituting "they" for the compound subject "the coach and the quarterback" results in "they understand."

COMPOUND SUBJECT JOINED BY *OR* OR *NOR* When parts of a subject are joined by *or* or *nor*, the verb agrees with the closer noun.

➤ Neither my mother nor my other relatives *are* happy with the decision.

➤ Either the administrators or the union *is* to blame.

INDEFINITE PRONOUNS AS SUBJECTS **Indefinite pronouns** refer to nonspecific individuals (*anybody, anyone, each, either, everybody, everyone, everything, neither, none, no one, somebody, someone, something*) and, hence, seem to be plural. However, most are singular.

➤ Everyone *likes* English.

➤ None of us *carries* a tune.

Note: There is a tendency to use the plural possessive-pronoun form *their* to refer to indefinite pronouns, since it conveniently refers to both males and females. Most teachers and editors, however, still expect the standard rule for agreement to be followed—hence, the need for *his or her*, as in "Everyone should turn in his or her final draft." Of course, one could be more precise and say, "Students should turn in their final drafts."

Some indefinite pronouns are always plural (*few, many*).

➤ Many *are called*, but few *are chosen*.

Some indefinite pronouns (*all, any, some*) are either singular or plural, depending on the noun or pronoun to which they refer.

> All of the students [plural] *like* English.

> All of the water [singular] *is* gone.

COLLECTIVE NOUNS AS SUBJECTS Most **collective nouns** (nouns that refer to a group) are considered singular.

> The *class has selected* her president.

> The *group wants* to remain seated.

Numerical collective nouns are either singular or plural, depending on whether the focus of the sentence is on the group or on the individual members of the group.

> A *majority* of team members *have* injuries.

> A *majority* of team members *has* selected Barbara as captain.

In the first sentence, the focus is on the many team members who have injuries. In the second, the team members in the majority are considered as a unit.

REVERSED SUBJECTS AND VERBS The verb must agree with its grammatical subject, even when the subject appears after the verb. When the subject of a sentence is placed after the verb, identifying the subject can be tricky. Remember that expressions such as *there is* and *there are* do not contain the subject.

There are twelve function keys, not ten, on my new computer.

Reckless driving and speeding was the explanation for the

traffic ticket.

SENTENCES WITH SUBJECT COMPLEMENTS A **subject complement** is a word or group of words that substitutes for the subject. A subject complement can easily be mistaken for the subject since it renames the subject.

> The *main requirement* of the job *is* a commitment to music and a demonstration of that commitment through station programming.

The verb "is" agrees with the singular subject "main requirement," not with the subject complement "commitment to music and a demonstration of that commitment through station programming."

VERBS AFTER *THAT, WHICH,* AND *WHO* The relative pronouns *that, which,* and *who* can be either singular or plural, depending on their **antecedents**—the word or words to which they refer.

> ➤ Students are one of the groups [plural] who are suffering from reductions in federal programs.

> ➤ A student [singular] who is ill should go to the health center.

It is not always immediately obvious if the antecedent is singular or plural. In the following examples, "one of the" creates a plural meaning; "only one of the" creates a singular meaning.

> ➤ The quality of the olive oil is *one of the* things [plural] that make some Italian dishes better than others.

Hint: To figure out what the verb should be, isolate the one word that can substitute for the subject—in this case "things"—and mentally state the simplified sentence that results: "Things make dishes better."

> ➤ *Only one of the* [singular] ingredients is worth mentioning—olive oil.

SINGULAR NOUNS ENDING IN *-S* Words that end in *-s* such as *academics, statistics, mathematics,* and *physics* are frequently singular.

> ➤ At some schools, *athletics is* stressed more than studying.

> ➤ *Statistics is* feared by many a graduate student.

A title containing plural nouns is singular.

> ➤ *Great Expectations* is still widely read in school.

Use the plural form when suggesting separate activities or characteristics.

> ➤ The statistics of war are shocking.

18b Irregular Verbs

Verbs change form to show changes in tense or time. Regular verbs form their past tense and past participle by adding *-d, -ed,* or *-t.* Irregular verbs form their past tense and past participle in many different ways. Irregular verb forms must be memorized. The following table gives the past tense and past participle of some common irregular verbs.

Common Irregular Verbs

PRESENT TENSE	PAST TENSE	PAST PARTICIPLE
arise	arose	arisen
awake	awoke, awaked	awaked, awoke
be	was, were	been
beat	beat	beaten, beat
become	became	become
begin	began	begun
bend	bent	bent
bite	bit	bitten, bit
blow	blew	blown
break	broke	broken
bring	brought	brought
build	built	built
burst	burst	burst
buy	bought	bought
catch	caught	caught
choose	chose	chosen
cling	clung	clung
come	came	come
cost	cost	cost
deal	dealt	dealt
dig	dug	dug
dive	dived, dove	dived
do	did	done
drag	dragged	dragged
draw	drew	drawn
dream	dreamed, dreamt	dreamed, dreamt
drink	drank	drunk
drive	drove	driven
eat	ate	eaten
fall	fell	fallen
feel	felt	felt
fight	fought	fought
find	found	found
fly	flew	flown
forget	forgot	forgotten, forgot
freeze	froze	frozen
get	got	gotten, got
give	gave	given

PRESENT TENSE	PAST TENSE	PAST PARTICIPLE
go	went	gone
grow	grew	grown
hang (suspend)	hung	hung
hang (execute)	hanged	hanged
have	had	had
hear	heard	heard
hide	hid	hidden
hold	held	held
hurt	hurt	hurt
keep	kept	kept
know	knew	known
lay (put)	laid	laid
lead	led	led
lend	lent	lent
let (allow)	let	let
lie (recline)	lay	lain
lose	lost	lost
make	made	made
prove	proved	proved, proven
read	read	read
ride	road	ridden
ring	rang	rung
rise	rose	risen
run	ran	run
say	said	said
see	saw	seen
send	sent	sent
set (put)	set	set
shake	shook	shaken
shine	shone	shone
shoot	shot	shot
shrink	shrank	shrunk, shrunken
sing	sang	sung
sink	sank	sunk
sit (be seated)	sat	sat
slay	slew	slain
sleep	slept	slept
speak	spoke	spoken
spin	spun	spun
spring	sprang	sprung
stand	stood	stood
steal	stole	stolen
sting	stung	stung

PRESENT TENSE	PAST TENSE	PAST PARTICIPLE
strike	struck	struck, stricken
swear	swore	sworn
swim	swam	swum
swing	swung	swung
take	took	taken
teach	taught	taught
throw	threw	thrown
wake	woke, waked	waked, woken
wear	wore	worn
wring	wrung	wrung
write	wrote	written

18c Auxiliary (Helping) Verbs

Auxiliary, **or helping**, **verbs** help to form different tenses. There are twenty-three helping verbs, some of which can also function as main verbs and others of which can only function as helping verbs.

**C
H
E
C
K
L
I
S
T
19**

Auxiliary Verbs That Function as Main Verbs or Helping Verbs

AS MAIN VERBS OR HELPING VERBS
be, am, is, are, was, were, being, been
do, does, did
have, has, had

MAIN VERB   I *have* enough money.

HELPING VERB   I *have* enjoyed my work.

AS HELPING VERBS ONLY
can, will, shall, should, could, would, may, might, must

HELPING VERB   I *should* stay longer.

19 Pronoun Agreement

Pronouns—*she, he, it, them*, and so forth— are words that substitute for nouns. Pronouns must agree with their antecedents—the word or words to which they refer—and with the verb in the sentence by agreeing in number and case.

19a Pronoun-Antecedent Agreement

Use singular pronouns to refer to singular nouns and plural pronouns to refer to plural nouns.

> *Steve* argued for *his* position, but his *friends* preferred *their* own
> plans.

> *Everyone* voted for *his or her* favorite candidate.

"Everyone" is singular; therefore, "his" or "her" (singular pronouns) are used.

Singular and Plural Forms of Pronouns

	SINGULAR			
FIRST PERSON	I	me	my	mine
SECOND PERSON	you	you	your	yours
THIRD PERSON	he/she/it	him/her/it	his/her/its	his/her/its
	PLURAL			
FIRST PERSON	we	us	our	ours
SECOND PERSON	you	you	your	yours
THIRD PERSON	they	them	their	theirs

C
H
E
C
K
L
I
S
T
20

19b With the Conjunctions *And, Or,* and *Nor*

Use a plural pronoun to refer to two nouns or pronouns joined by *and*.

> ➤ *The instructor and the student* agreed that *they* should meet.

> ➤ *He and I* asked if *we* could collaborate on the next assignment.

Use a singular pronoun to refer to two singular nouns joined by *or* or *nor*.

> ➤ Either *Mark or Dave* can take *his* turn first.

If you have one singular and one plural noun joined by *or* or *nor*, place the plural second and use a plural pronoun.

> ➤ Neither *Ralph nor his three sisters* have received *their* checks.

19c Indefinite Pronoun Antecedents

Indefinite pronouns that are singular should be referred to by singular pronouns.

➤ *Each* of the colleges has *its* own admissions policy.

Some indefinite pronouns are plural (*both, few, many*) and require plural pronouns.

➤ A *few* of the players have yet to pass *their* physicals.

Some indefinite pronouns may be either singular or plural (*all, any, some*). A pronoun referring to one of these indefinite pronouns is singular if the indefinite pronoun referred to stresses the action of an entire group as a whole; it is plural if it refers to the various situations of members of the group.

➤ *Some* of the *book* was enjoyable.

➤ *Some* of the *costumes* are grotesque.

19d With Collective Nouns

Treat collective nouns (*class, team, audience, committee*, and so forth) as singular if you are stressing the group's acting as a unit; treat them as plural if you are stressing the actions of the group's individual members.

➤ The *class* will take *its* final exam on Monday.

➤ The *class* immediately began to register *their* protests.

Do not treat the same noun as both singular and plural in the same sentence.

➤ The *class* was stunned but then registered *their* protests.

REVISED   The students in the class were stunned but then registered their protests.

19e Gender-Inclusive Pronouns

When referring to a singular noun that may be either male or female, use *his or her*, not *his* alone. If you wish to avoid using *his or her* (which, when overused, can sound awkward), switch to the plural.

➤ A *doctor's* responsibility is to *his or her* patients.

REVISED   *Doctors* are responsible for *their* patients.

➤ A *parent* should take good care *of his* children.

REVISED   *Parents* should take good care of *their* children.

20 Pronoun Case

Pronouns must be used in the proper case form. **Case** refers to the way a pronoun functions in a sentence—as a subject (**nominative case**), as an object (**objective case**), or to show possession (**possessive case**).

➤ It is *she* who must be obeyed.

In this sentence, "she" functions as a subject complement (a word that completes the meaning of the subject and renames it) and must be in the nominative case.

➤ We elected *her* president.

"Her" is the object and thus is in the objective case.

➤ The president wanted to know if *her* changes to the agenda had been added.

"Her" shows possession.

Case Forms of Personal Pronouns

NOMINATIVE CASE	OBJECTIVE CASE	POSSESSIVE CASE
I	me	my
we	us	our
you	you	your
he/she/it	him/her/it	his/her/its
they	them	their

C
H
E
C
K
L
I
S
T
21

20a With Appositives

Appositives mean the same thing as the word to which they refer.

➤ Mr. Long, *my algebra teacher,* just retired.

Appositives and the nouns to which they refer (their antecedents) should be in the same case.

> The handout was for the only two freshmen in the class, Laura and *me*.

Hint: When you read the sentence to yourself, test it with only a pronoun in the appositive position. Listen to the sound of your sentence. You would not say: "The handout was for I." You would say: "The handout was for me."

Use the subjective case when the pronoun acts as a subject.

> Loyal friends, John and *I* decided to stay in spite of the rain.

> *I* decided to stay.

Use the objective case when the pronoun acts as an object.

> The lawyer asked the witnesses, Jane and *me*, to testify.

> The lawyer asked *me* to testify.

(See Checklist 20 for a review of how to form plural pronouns in different cases.)

20b With Incomplete Comparisons

When using pronouns to compare two nouns, avoid using incomplete sentence structures or elliptical constructions. Such sentences omit words and require careful use of pronouns. Be sure sentences convey the meaning that you intend them to convey.

> John likes sailing more than I.

This sentence means that John likes sailing more than I like sailing. The writer has omitted "more than I like sailing."

> John likes sailing more than me.

This sentence means that John likes sailing more than he likes me. The writer has omitted "more than he likes me."

20c With Subjects of Infinitives

Subjects of infinitives should be in the objective case.

> We wanted *him* to see the photographs.

"Him" is the subject of the infinitive phrase "him to see the photographs." *Hint:* First identify the subject and the verb: "We wanted." Next identify the object by asking, Who or what did we want? The answer: "him to see the photographs." The entire phrase is the object of the sentence. The object happens to include its own subject—"him."

20d Before Gerunds

Pronouns before **gerunds** (*-ing* words used as nouns) must be in the possessive case.

> *His* walking away showed good judgment.

The "walking away" is owned by him. To show ownership, use the possessive case.

Sometimes an *-ing* word preceded by a pronoun is not a gerund phrase, but a participial phrase. Consider the following sentence:

> I saw *him* walking away.

In this sentence, the object is "him," which is modified by "walking away," a participial phrase.

20e Pronoun Reference

Pronoun reference in a sentence must be clear. Readers should have no trouble figuring out to whom or to what a pronoun refers. Revise sentences with ambiguous references, even if you have to repeat a reference rather than use the pronoun.

> AMBIGUOUS   Americans admire movie stars because *they* are
> wealthy and attractive.

> REVISED   Americans admire movie stars because *movie stars*
> are wealthy and attractive.

In the first sentence, "they" can refer to either "Americans" or "movie stars."

> AMBIGUOUS   The new prison has updated facilities, but *they* still
> treat inmates harshly.

> REVISED   The new prison has updated facilities, but the prison
> officials still treat inmates harshly.

Grammatically, "they" refers to "facilities" in the first sentence. Actually, "they" refers to "the prison officials," which is implied but not mentioned in that sentence.

PRONOUN REFERENCE WITH RELATIVE PRONOUNS *That, which, who, whoever, whom, whomever,* and *whose* are **relative pronouns**, pronouns that relate or connect parts of sentences. Use *who* or *whom* to refer to people; use *that* to refer to objects. Informally, *that* is sometimes used to refer to a class of people.

> I surprised *whoever* was there.

"Whoever" is the subject of the clause "was there."

> She was the only one in the class *who* had been to France.

> The place *that* she wanted to see was France.

Note: Use *who* or *whoever* in the subject position of a sentence; use *whom* or *whomever* if the pronoun functions as an object. When you want to refer to one or more things rather than to people, use *which* or *that.*

> The antiques *that* we bought in Maine are from the eighteenth century.

The clause "that we bought in Maine" is an essential clause (see the next section) and should not be set off with commas.

> Our antiques, *which* are primarily in the upstairs rooms, do not match the style of our contemporary home.

The clause "which are primarily in the upstairs rooms" is a nonessential clause (see the next section) and must be set off with commas.

PRONOUN REFERENCE WITH *THAT* AND *WHICH* IN ESSENTIAL AND NONESSENTIAL CLAUSES Use *that* to introduce expressions that are essential to the meaning of a sentence. Use *which* to introduce nonessential expressions. Remember to set off nonessential clauses with commas.

> The game *that* I remember best was the only one we lost.

In this sentence, the writer wants to make a point that of all the games he or she remembers, there is one that stands out.

> The game, *which* I remember well, was the only one we lost.

In this sentence, the *which* expression is presented as an afterthought, something not essential to the meaning of the sentence. The commas set the idea aside, much as parentheses do.

Avoid using *that* or *which* to refer to a general state of affairs implied, but not necessarily specified, in your writing.

➤ I was concerned ~~that~~ [because] you had not called.

➤ ~~That~~ [This sentence] needs to be revised.

21 Adjectives and Adverbs

21a Adjectives

Adjectives modify nouns and pronouns. They can be words, phrases, or clauses. Adjectives usually follow verb forms of *be*, *seem*, *appear*, and *become*; sensory words such as *taste*, *touch*, and *feel*; and a few other verbs, including *grow*, *prove*, *get*, *keep*, *remain*, and *turn*.

➤ I am *happy*.

➤ It tastes *good*.

➤ She has been proved *wrong*.

21b Adverbs

Adverbs modify verbs, adjectives, and other adverbs. Adverbs can be a single word, a phrase, or a clause. Adverbs are often formed by adding *-ly* to adjectives.

➤ It rained *softly*.

➤ It rained *in the evening*.

➤ *When it rained*, we went inside.

Sometimes the same word can function as either an adverb or an adjective, depending on its meaning in a sentence.

➤ She is feeling *well*.

"Well" (meaning "healthy") is an adjective, modifying the subject.

➤ She did *well* on the test.

"Well" is an adverb modifying the verb.

21c Comparatives and Superlatives

Adverbs and adjectives have three forms: the **positive form** (which is the adverb or adjective itself), the **comparative form** (which compares two things), and the **superlative form** (which compares three or more things). In general, form the comparative or the superlative by adding *-er* and *-est* to the base.

➤ I drive *faster* than Roy.

➤ Tina drives the *fastest*.

With words ending in *-ly*, however, the comparative and superlative are formed by adding the words *more* and *most* (or *less* and *least*) before the adverb.

➤ She drives *more quickly*.

POSITIVE	COMPARATIVE	SUPERLATIVE
fast	faster	fastest
quickly	more quickly	most quickly

With longer adjectives, the comparative and superlative are also formed by adding *more* and *most* (or *less* and *least*) before the adjective.

➤ the *most beautiful* view.

POSITIVE	COMPARATIVE	SUPERLATIVE
pretty	prettier	prettiest
beautiful	more beautiful	most beautiful

22 Grammar Tips for Speakers of English As a Second Language

Some features of the English language pose special difficulties to students whose native language is not English. This section addresses several problem areas.

22a Articles

Articles—*a, an, the*—indicate that the word following them is a noun. Articles can cause problems for nonnative speakers because the rules for their use have no equivalents in most other languages.

WHEN TO USE *A/AN* Use *a* or *an* with singular, countable nouns that are unknown to the reader or listener. Use *a* before countable nouns that begin with a consonant; use *an* before countable nouns that begin with a vowel and before countable nouns that begin with a silent *h*.

➤ *a* cat, *a* ticket, *a* house; *an* owl, *an* exit, *an* honor

➤ I would like to buy *a* ticket to New York.

➤ I looked for *an* exit but did not see one.

WHEN TO USE *THE*

1. Use *the* to indicate a noun, singular or plural, that is already known to a reader or listener.

   ➤ ~~A~~ *The* ticket is in my bag.

   "A ticket" implies that there is a ticket, but we don't know what its purpose is. "The ticket" demonstrates that the ticket is known to us.

   ➤ ~~Tickets~~ *The tickets* are in my bag.

   ➤ I looked for ~~an~~ *the* exit but did not see it.

2. With singular, uncountable nouns, use *the*, not *a* or *an*.

   ➤ ~~A~~ *The* milk is in the refrigerator.

WHEN NOT TO USE AN ARTICLE

1. With singular, proper nouns that refer to a specific place, do not use an article.

   ➤ ~~the~~ Atlanta; ~~the~~ Washington, D.C.

   Note: "The" is used with some large geographic areas: *the South, the West Coast, the United States.*

2. When you want to indicate a general category, do not use an article.

   ➤ ~~The~~ *Car emissions* ~~car emissions~~ can pollute the environment.

   The original sentence implies that a specific type of car emission can pollute the environment.

   ➤ ~~The~~ *Men* ~~men~~ and ~~the~~ women approach conflict differently.

The original sentence implies specific men and women, not men and women generally.

22b Verbs

Verbs can cause problems for speakers of English as a second language. This section highlights a few areas that are especially difficult. (See pages 124–130 for a more thorough review of verbs.)

GERUNDS AND INFINITIVES   Two verb forms that often cause problems are gerunds and infinitives. Gerunds are *-ing* words used as nouns; infinitives consist of the word *to* plus the base form of the verb. When deciding whether to use a gerund or an infinitive, keep the following in mind:

1. Use a gerund, not an infinitive, as the object of a preposition. *Reminder:* Prepositions are words such as *after*, *before*, *by*, *for*, and *of*. Use *-ing* words after prepositions.

   ➤ It is satisfying to work hard *before resting*.

   ➤ Her reason *for leaving* just before dinner was not clear.

   ➤ She saw the play *after reading* the novel.

2. Infinitives are usually used after nouns, participles, adjectives, and verbs.

   ➤ I find it satisfying *to rest* after a hard day's work.

   ➤ Her decision *to leave* just before dinner was puzzling.

   There is one exception to this general rule: verbs that express emotion such as love and hate can be followed by either a gerund or an infinitive.

   ➤ I love *hiking*.

   ➤ I love *to hike*.

   ➤ I hate *decorating* a tree on Christmas Eve.

   ➤ I hate *to decorate* a tree on Christmas Eve.

3. Follow some verbs with a gerund, *not* an infinitive.

   ➤ I enjoy *hiking*.

   ➤ We finished *decorating* our tree on Christmas Eve.

   ➤ I dislike *exercising*.

   ➤ I don't mind *dancing*.

PARTICIPLES A **present participle** is a form of a verb that ends in *-ing*; it tells how something or someone is, was, or will be acting. A **past participle** ends in either *-d*, *-ed*, *-en*, *-n*, or *-t*; it tells how something or someone is, was, or will be acted upon.

1. Use the present-participle form when the subject acts.

   ➤ My car is *running* well.

   ➤ The trip was *exciting*.

2. Use the past-participle form when the subject is acted upon.

   ➤ My car was *wrecked*.

   ➤ The wood was *burned*.

For a list of irregular verbs and their past-participle forms, see pages 128–130.

HELPING VERBS A helping verb must come before the base form of the main verb or before the infinitive form of the verb. For a list of helping verbs, see Checklist 19.

➤ She *has* helped me for many years.

➤ They *must* learn how to study.

➤ We *might have* left earlier, but the roads were icy.

Do is used as a helping verb to form questions and to form negative statements.

➤ *Did* you enjoy your trip to Mexico?

➤ My sister *did not* travel with me to Mexico.

➤ The snow *does not* look cold.

After *do* and some helping verbs (such as *can*, *could*, *may*, or *might*), a verb is often used alone, without sentence modifiers following it. Note that there is no *-s* added to the verbs "care" or "happen."

➤ She does *care*.

➤ It could *happen*.

22c Complete Sentences

In some languages, one word can serve as both subject and predicate. In English, only imperative sentences can omit the subject (the subject, "you," is understood). Other sentences require both a subject and a verb.

➤ *Look* at the stop sign.

➤ *Jump* higher.

➤ ~~Bought~~ I bought a ticket.

➤ ~~Started~~ I started skiing lessons.

➤ The animals were outside in the cold.

➤ My uncle is a radio announcer.

When the subject follows the verb, an expletive (*there is, there are, it is,* and so forth) is usually required.

➤ It is usually cold in Minnesota.

Introductory words can sometimes confuse nonnative speakers into omitting expletives.

➤ Although we were comfortable, it was always cold in Minnesota.

Do not omit the verb in sentences like

➤ The Coca-Cola museum in Atlanta is worth visiting.

➤ He is a very good cook.

Punctuation

Punctuation marks play both stylistic and structural roles in sentences. The choice of punctuation marks is often critical to the way readers react to a writer's ideas. Punctuation marks help clarify the meaning of a sentence, telling a reader when to pause, when to slow down, and when to move ahead. The structural roles of punctuation marks in sentences include indicating sentence boundaries, separating sentence parts, and showing that letters are omitted.

23 End Punctuation

Every sentence must end with either a period, a question mark, or an exclamation point.

23a The Period [.]

Use a period at the end of statements, mild commands, or indirect questions.

> ➤ The banks are closed today.

> ➤ Never touch the exposed magnetic surface of the disk.

> ➤ I wonder what happened to him.

23b The Question Mark [?]

Use a question mark at the end of direct questions and within parentheses and dashes to indicate uncertainty within a sentence.

> ➤ What happened to him?

> ➤ It was early (before 6 a.m.?).

23c The Exclamation Point [!]

Use an exclamation point at the end of assertions of surprise or other strong emotions.

> ➤ "He's alive!" Dr. Frankenstein screamed.

> ➤ Don't touch that disk! The disk drive is spinning.

Do not overuse exclamation points. Reserve them for special effects such as in the above examples.

24 The Comma [,]

Writers use commas to signal pauses within sentences and to clarify structure.

24a With Coordinating Conjunctions in Compound Sentences

Unless the sentences are short, use a comma between two independent clauses joined by a coordinating conjunction (*and, but, for, nor, or, so, yet*) to signal the end of one clause and the beginning of the next.

> ➤ The judge listened attentively, but many of the jurors had trouble following the testimony.

The comma can be omitted in short, parallel sentences.

> ➤ The judge listened attentively but many of the jurors did not.

A comma is *not* used when a coordinating conjunction links the parts of a compound verb.

> ➤ The judge listened attentively / but ruled against the motion.

24b After Most Introductory Material

Use a comma after introductory material to signal to the reader that the main part of the sentence is beginning. The comma may be omitted if the introductory material is brief and flows directly into the main clause.

> ➤ Nevertheless, we decided to continue.

> ➤ Although most film critics disliked the movie, it enjoyed great success at the box office.

➤ In some cities the movie enjoyed great success at the box office.

24c Between Items in a Series

A comma is used to separate each item in a series. Usually, *and* or *or* is used before the last item.

➤ I am studying statistics, astronomy, and physics.

➤ Next term, I plan to take algebra, chemistry, or geology.

Each item in a series can itself consist of many words.

➤ The mayor was delighted that the city council approved the new parking garage, defeated changes in the zoning ordinance, and delayed consideration of increases in sewerage rates.

When each item in a series includes commas, a semicolon is used to separate the items.

➤ The mayor was delighted that the city council approved the new parking garage, the one to be built near city hall; defeated changes in the zoning ordinance, changes that would have helped save many old neighborhoods; and delayed consideration of increases in sewerage rates.

A series may consist of only two words, as in the case of coordinate (or reversible) adjectives before a noun.

➤ *Halloween* is a suspenseful, terrifying movie.

   or

➤ *Halloween* is a terrifying, suspenseful movie.

Do not use a comma with adjectives whose order in a sequence is not reversible.

➤ We saw a new Australian movie.

The adjectives "new" and "Australian" are not reversible. You would not say "an Australian new movie."

24d Before and After Nonessential Words and Phrases

Use a pair of commas to indicate that the words between the commas are nonessential and could be omitted without loss of meaning. Nonessential material may be informative or interesting, but it is always extra information, not information that narrows and, thus, helps to identify the subject under consideration.

Remember two things when using commas to distinguish between essential and nonessential material: (1) always use a pair of commas to separate nonessential material, one on each side of the material, and (2) when in doubt about whether something is nonessential or not, leave the commas out.

➤ Graduates *who are adept at using computers* have an advantage in the job market.

The example above assumes that these graduates have an advantage over those graduates who are not adept at using computers.

➤ Graduates, *who are adept at using computers*, have an advantage in the job market.

That is, these graduates have this particular advantage over nongraduates. The information about their computer skills is offered here as something extra; the sentence can be read without the words between the commas.

24e Other Comma Rules

Some comma rules do not fit into categories. Think of these rules as ones that apply in only certain circumstances.

1. Use commas to prevent misreading.

   ➤ Soon after, Bill left the room.

2. Use commas to indicate omitted words.

   ➤ Tim donated $50; Robert, $100.

3. Use commas to set off the year when the month and day are also given.

   ➤ The hearing was set for May 12, 1987, but it actually began in July.

4. Use commas to set off the name of a state, county, or country that follows the name of a city.

   ➤ Our Mobile, Alabama, location has three stores to serve you.

5. Use commas with contrasting expressions (*but, not, rather than*) that emphasize a sense of contrast.

   ➤ The managers promoted Joan, rather than Mike.

24f Comma Problems

1. Do not be fooled by the pause and punctuate the subject of a sentence as an introductory phrase.

   ➤ To format a disk ⁄ requires one simple command.

2. Do not use a comma between compound verbs (verbs joined by *or* or *and*).

   ➤ We studied for the test ⁄ and developed our confidence.

   Commas should not be used to separate compound verbs; in this sentence, "studied" and "developed" are compound verbs.

3. Do not use commas inconsistently.

   ➤ Since it is a beautiful day ‸ think I'll go for a walk. Because

   I have little time ‸ rarely exercise during the work week.

   If you use a comma after an introductory phrase, do so consistently throughout your paper.

4. Although commas should be used to separate the non-essential material from the rest of the sentence, do not use a comma to separate two complete sentences.

   ➤ Talk is cheap, ~~action~~ . Action ‸ is what counts.

   ➤ You shouldn't be concerned about grammar as you draft, ‸
   ~~you~~ You ‸ should focus on content and organization.

5. Do not forget the second comma in nonessential phrases.

   Think of these two commas is if they were parentheses.

   ➤ Computer viruses, often compared to physical diseases , ‸

   are common on our campus.

25 The Semicolon [;] and Colon [:]

25a The Semicolon [;]

In addition to using the semicolon between series items with internal commas (see page 146), the semicolon can be used to separate closely connected independent clauses that are not connected by conjunctions. The basic rule in using semicolons

Quick Review of Comma Rules

USE A COMMA

- between two independent clauses joined by one of the seven coordinating conjunctions: *and, but, for, nor, or, so, yet.*
- after most introductory material.
- between coordinate items in a series.
- before and after nonessential words and phrases.
- as called for according to convention or to prevent misreading.

is to be sure that you have complete sentences (independent clauses) on both sides of the semicolon.

> The rain never ceased; it continued throughout the night and into the next week.

> Time went quickly; as a result, before she knew it, she was too old to find a good job.

Hence, however, indeed, moreover, still, therefore, thus, and similar terms are adverbs (sometimes called **conjunctive adverbs**) that belong entirely to the second sentence. Therefore, they cannot be used like a coordinating conjunction to join two sentences. When used after a semicolon, they are followed by a comma. When used as interrupters within independent clauses, they are set off with commas.

> Dan found it difficult to beg forgiveness; however, Roseanne eventually forgave him.

> Dan found it difficult to beg forgiveness; Roseanne, however, eventually forgave him.

25b Semicolon Problems

Do not use a semicolon in sentences that do not contain two independent clauses. Use a comma instead.

> The interview went well; better than I expected.

The phrase "better than I expected" is not an independent clause. It is a phrase that modifies the entire sentence and that can be separated from the sentence with a comma.

> As time passed; I knew I was going to like her.

The first part of the sentence is an introductory clause (acting as an adverb) and must be connected to the independent clause with a comma.

25c The Colon [:]

Within a sentence, a colon announces a list, a question, or a complete sentence that follows.

1. Use a colon after an independent clause to introduce a list, a direct quotation, or an explanation.

   ➤ These are the key factors to consider when purchasing software: price, performance, and support.

   ➤ Confucius says: "It is easy to be rich and not haughty; it is difficult to be poor and not grumble."

   ➤ When the time is right, you'll know it: you'll be ready to get married, and you'll want to do it without delay.

2. Use a colon after salutations in formal business letters.

   ➤ Dear Ms. Bartholemew:

   ➤ Dear Dr. Smith:

   ➤ Dear Admissions Committee:

   ➤ Dear Personnel Officer:

   Instead of saying "Dear Sir or Madam," use a noun to substitute for the person to whom you are addressing the letter.

3. Use a colon to separate the title of a work from the subtitle.

   ➤ *Conrad Richter: The Novelist as Philosopher*

   ➤ *A Writer's Tool: The Computer in Composition Instruction*

25d Colon Problems

1. Do not use a colon when a period or other punctuation is more appropriate.

   ➤ We bought enough paper to last for several years: ~~paper~~ . Paper

   for laser printers is less expensive when you buy it in

   quantity.

In this case, the two sentences are not sufficiently linked to justify using a colon.

2. Do not use a colon to separate a verb from its objects or complements.

➤ Three factors to consider when purchasing software are: price, performance, and support.

or

➤ When purchasing software, consider these three factors: price, performance, and support.

26 The Apostrophe [']

The apostrophe has two different functions: it indicates possession (ownership), and it indicates omission of a letter or of letters (in contractions). Mastering a few standard rules for apostrophe use can help you detect and diagnose many common errors.

26a Indicating Possession

With singular nouns, add -'s.

➤ The woman's briefcase was stolen.

With plural nouns ending in -s, add an apostrophe only.

➤ The two countries' flags fly side by side.

With plural nouns not ending in -s, add -'s.

➤ The children's bikes were left in the driveway.

With compound nouns, add -'s to the last element.

➤ My brother-in-law's hammering went on until dusk.

With compound nouns indicating *joint* ownership, add -'s to the last element.

➤ Bob and Mary's portrait hangs above their fireplace mantle.

If there are two or more *separate* owners, add -'s to each noun.

➤ Our son's and daughter's dating habits are baffling.

When a singular or plural name ends in -*s*, add either -'*s* or add an apostrophe only.

> ➤ Charles's book is on the desk.

> *or*

> ➤ Charles' book is on the desk.

> ➤ The Douglas's house is in the country.

> *or*

> ➤ The Douglas' house is in the country.

Note: Convention calls for *Zeus'*, *Moses'*, and *Jesus'*, as well as a single apostrophe with names like *Euripides* that are difficult to pronounce with an added syllable.

26b Indicating Omission

In contractions.

> ➤ *We're* going home because *I've* got a cold.

Informally, in dates.

> ➤ The fall of '93 was surprisingly mild.

In standard or invented abbreviations.

> ➤ The story began on the front page, but the editor continued it on a later page, indicating the specific place with the words "cont'd, p. 3."

26c Other Uses of the Apostrophe

Use -'*s* to form the plural of lowercase letters, abbreviations containing periods, and words used as examples of words.

> ➤ add *x*'s

> ➤ compare I.D.'s

> ➤ too many *no*'s

Note: It is becoming acceptable to use -*s* only to form the plural of numbers and capital letters.

> ➤ 1960s

> ➤ the three Rs

Quick Review of Possessive Apostrophe Rules

SINGULAR

° Add -'s to singular nouns not ending in -s.

> the dog's collar

° Add -'s or a single apostrophe to singular nouns ending in -s.

> my friend Bess's [or Bess'] mother

PLURAL

° Add a single apostrophe or -'s to plural nouns ending in -s.

> the boys' clubhouse

° Add a single apostrophe or -'s to names.

> the Santos' house
> the Santos's house

° Add -'s to plural nouns not ending in s.

> our children's friends

COMPOUND NOUNS

° In general, add -'s to the last element.

> my son-in-law's wife

° Add -'s to the last element to show joint possession.

> Abbott and Costello's comedy routines

° Add -'s to each element if there are two or more owners.

> Roberta's and Carol's tastes were very different.

26d Common Errors with Apostrophes

Many people confuse the possessive form *its* ("belonging to it") with the contraction *it's* ("it is" or "it has"). Similarly, people sometimes confuse the possessive *your* ("belonging to you") with the contraction *you're* ("you are"). Whenever you use any of these forms, check your sentence to determine whether you have used the correct form. Read the sentence, substituting the full phrase (*you are, it has, it is*) for the contraction (*you're, it's*).

If the sentence does not make sense, then you know that you have to revise it.

> *It's* It's fur stood on end when the dog came into the room.

The sentence "It has fur stood on end" does not make sense.

Or you may have to substitute the contraction (or the uncontracted form of the word) for the possessive pronoun.

> *It's* Its been a long time since we met.

27 Quotation Marks [" "]

27a Quoting Exact Words

1. Use quotation marks to indicate someone's exact words, whether written, spoken, or thought.

   > She said, "I'm happy that the course is almost over."

2. Use single quotation marks ['. . .'] to indicate a quotation within a quotation.

   > She said, "I want you to remember that Frost's poem 'Out, Out' contains an allusion to Shakespeare's *Macbeth.*"

3. Use indention, instead of quotation marks, for quoting more than four typed lines of continuous prose or more than three printed lines. Shorter passages of poetry can also be indented for emphasis.

   > The best part of her talk related to the uses of the Internet for E-mail:
   >> If students are going to benefit from their access to e-mail, then they have to learn how to do more than send and receive mail. They need to learn how to subscribe to lists, how to print text from screen, and how to create groups of students to whom they can mail their text. (Hawisher 386)

27b Formal Definitions

Use quotation marks to indicate formal definitions or words not to be taken at face value.

> *Intrepid* means "bold" or "fearless."

> Then this "genius" forgot the keys.

Punctuating Direct Quotations

- When a direct quotation is followed by a "tag" (*he said, she said*, and so forth), place the punctuation inside the quotation marks.

  ➤ "Let's take a closer look," she said.

- When a direct quotation is interrupted by a tag, set off the tag with a pair of commas, inserting the first comma before the first close quotation mark.

  ➤ "May I," she asked, "take a closer look?"

- With a somewhat lengthy quotation, use a colon rather than a comma to introduce it.

  ➤ There are, according to Joseph Weizenbaum, severe limits on what we should ask of computers: "Since we do not have any ways of making computers wise, we ought not now to give computers tasks that demand wisdom."

- Semicolons are placed *outside* close quotation marks.

  ➤ You said, "The check is in the mail"; I can only respond, "Not in my mail."

- Colons are placed *outside* close quotation marks.

  ➤ In Jim's words, these are his "four basic food groups": burgers, pizza, fried chicken, and beer.

- Periods and commas are placed inside quotation marks.

  ➤ The speech ended with the words "I rest my case."

- When the quoted sentence ends in a question mark or an exclamation point, no comma is used.

  ➤ "May I take a closer look?" she asked.

- When the entire sentence is a question, a question mark is placed *outside* close quotation marks.

  ➤ What does the last line mean: "And miles to go before I sleep"?

- Quotations longer than four typed lines should be set off from the rest of your essay without quotation marks (unless they occur *within* the passage). Indent the quoted passage an additional half inch or five spaces on the left side only (total indention: ten spaces).

27c Titles

Use quotation marks for titles of short works that are not part of a collection, individual items (stories, short poems, articles, songs, essays, and so forth) that usually appear in collections, episodes of radio and television shows, and subdivisions of a book.

➤ "A Rose for Emily" is a famous story by William Faulkner.

➤ "Why I Want a Wife" is an essay by Judy Syfers.

➤ I enjoyed the episode "Family Business" from *Star Trek: Deep Space Nine*.

➤ The chapter "The Creation of Sentences" was very helpful.

27d Quotations within Sentences

Except for quotation marks, quotations integrated into sentences do not require additional punctuation.

➤ He knows that someday "things will even out."

Do not use quotation marks in indirect discourse.

➤ His only reply was that someday he would get even.

28 Other Punctuation Marks

28a The Dash [—]

Some software programs allow you to create a dash. Otherwise, create a dash by typing two hyphens, one after the other, with no space before or after them.

The dash is used to emphasize a shift in tone or thought or to announce a list, a restatement, or an amplification—all matters that could be handled with other punctuation marks but with a slightly different effect. If used judiciously, dashes can help writers control the way their words are received by readers. Use a dash to get a reader's attention. A pair of dashes can be used in the middle of a sentence to emphasize—by setting off—an insertion in the middle of the sentence. Dashes are less formal than commas, but used in pairs they can serve a similar purpose.

➤ At the conference sat Roosevelt, Churchill, and Stalin—the leaders of the war against Hitler.

➤ He had practiced hard for the recital—did anyone else realize how hard?—yet he was still nervous.

28b Parentheses [( )]

Parentheses are used to separate (or set aside) words or phrases from the rest of a sentence. Readers assume that the words between the parentheses are supplementary, intended to comment on or clarify a point. Occasionally, entire sentences are placed in parentheses to signal to a reader that additional information is being provided.

Use parentheses sparingly; substitute paired commas in those cases in which you want an additional comment to be more closely linked to the main flow of the sentence.

➤ Our local newspaper (at least it purports to be a newspaper) uncovered corruption.

1. Use parentheses to define terms that a reader cannot be expected to know.

   ➤ Several epidemiologists (scientists who study epidemics) were called in to assess the danger of rabies in the city.

2. Use parentheses to note a point that you would like a reader to consider, even though it is not essential to the gist of your text.

   ➤ A knowledge of computer programming (no longer thought to be an essential component of computer literacy) can enhance a technical writer's credibility with engineers.

3. Use parentheses to enclose in-text citations.

   ➤ Norton's *Textra Extra* (McFarland 1994) includes many handy tips about word processing.

28c Ellipses [. . .]

Ellipsis points are three equally spaced dots used to indicate that something in a passage is missing, such as part of a writer's exact words in a quotation. Note that you need one space after each dot.

Use ellipsis points in a documented paper when you want to omit material from a long quotation. Use ellipsis points only in the middle of a quote and at the end. Take care not to distort the meaning of the original text through your use of ellipsis points: if the text says that "Movie X was technically flawed and not enjoyable," do not write, "Movie X was . . . enjoyable."

➤ I disagree with the argument that the "students of the twenty-first century . . . will rarely use pencil and paper."

Use of ellipsis points also indicates that something is unfinished; it is acceptable—if it is not overused—in informal writing.

➤ And that's the way things went for me. . . .

28d Square Brackets [ ]

Square brackets are used to enclose words that you, as editor, have inserted into a quote for the purpose of clarity or to produce a grammatically correct sentence.

➤ Then the speaker concluded: "Our efforts at such [campaign-financing] reforms have never appeared more promising."

Brackets are also used around parenthetical material within parentheses.

➤ These nudes are clearly Rubenesque (after the Flemish painter Peter Paul Rubens [1577–1640]).

The Latin term *sic* ("thus") is traditionally used inside brackets to indicate an obvious error in the original source, although at times it is more helpful just to give the correct form inside brackets.

➤ The sign said: This sail [*sic*] ends tomorrow.

28e The Slash [/]

The slash can be used to indicate alternative words of equal weight.

➤ Each student has his/her own computer.

Do not use *his/her* or *he/she* constructions routinely, however, since they generally distract your readers. To avoid referring to the generic pronoun *he*, rewrite the above sentence, using the plural.

➤ All of the students have their own computers.

A slash is also used to indicate lines of poetry when they are not indented, but are run into the text. Be sure to put a space before and after the slash.

> ➤ I've often wondered what Robert Frost meant by repeating the last two lines of "Stopping by Woods on a Snowy Evening": "And miles to go before I sleep, / And miles to go before I sleep."

Mechanics

29 Capitalization

Academic writing tasks require correct use of capital letters. Use these guidelines, and consult a dictionary when you have questions.

29a The First Word in a Sentence

The first word in a sentence must be capitalized. If you quote a complete sentence, you must capitalize the first word in the quotation.

➤ According to Tosca Moon Lee, "Even wiring private homes with the fiber-optic cable that will be necessary for such a quick exchange of high amounts of information could cost $100 billion."

29b Proper Nouns and Modifiers Derived from Them

A **proper noun** is a noun that names a specific person, place, or thing. Capitalize all proper nouns.

➤ *President Siegel* asked students to work on flood-relief efforts.

➤ *Atlanta* was not affected by the flood of 1994.

➤ *Canada* was settled by both the *English* and the *French*.

➤ *The Kennesaw State College Student Government Association* established a flood-relief committee.

Modifiers derived from proper nouns are usually capitalized.

➤ Delegates from twenty *African* countries met at the United Nations.

"African" is a modifier created by adding *-n* to the proper noun.

➤ The *Canadian* parliament is modeled on parliament structures in place in Great Britain.

29c Titles of Works

Capitalize the first and last words in a title and all other words except conjunctions, articles, and prepositions of four letters or less.

> ➤ *The Night Before Christmas*

> ➤ *The Bluest Eye*

> ➤ "Battle Hymn of the Republic"

29d Personal Titles

1. Titles used before personal names must be capitalized.

   > ➤ My orthodontist is *Dr.* Ross.

   > ➤ Former *President* Richard Nixon's record was tarnished by the Watergate incident.

   > ➤ I'll always remember *Aunt* Maria.

However, titles used after personal names are usually lowercase.

> ➤ Daniel Patrick Moynihan, the Democratic senator from New York

2. Titles that refer to a high position may be capitalized, even when they are used without the name of the person holding the title.

   > ➤ the Pope

   > ➤ the President

   > ➤ the Director

29e Other Capitalization Rules

THE FIRST WORD IN LINES OF POETRY Capitalize the first word in each line of a poem, whether or not the poetic line forms a complete sentence, unless the author has intentionally chosen *not* to capitalize the words.

> ➤ Whose woods these are I think I know

> ➤ anyone lived in a pretty how town

In the second example, "anyone" should not be capitalized because E. E. Cummings, the author, did not capitalize this line, the first line of his poem "anyone lived in a pretty how town."

SPECIFIC SCHOOL OR COLLEGE COURSES Capitalize the specific title of a course. Do not capitalize the names of courses if you are referring to them generally rather than specifically, except for language courses.

➤ My *art* course is *Art 301*. My *French* course is *French 350*.

➤ I'm taking two *English* courses: *English Literature* and *History of the English Language*.

29f Capitalization Errors

Do not capitalize the following:

1. The words *a*, *an*, and *the* when used with proper nouns

   ➤ a Democrat

   ➤ the *New Yorker*

2. The seasons of the year

   ➤ the fall semester

3. The decades

   ➤ the twenties

C H E C K L I S T 25

Quick Review of Capitalization Rules

ALWAYS CAPITALIZE
* the first word in a sentence.
* all proper nouns.
* titles used before personal names.
* the specific title of a course.

USUALLY CAPITALIZE
* modifiers derived from proper nouns.
* the first word in a line of poetry.

---

30 Italics (Underlining), Abbreviations, Numbers

30a Italics for Titles of Full-Length Works

Italicize or underline titles of full-length works, including books, periodicals, films, TV or radio shows, works of visual art, plays, poems published separately as books, and so forth.

➤ *Murphy Brown*

➤ the *Washington Post*

➤ Picasso's *Guernica*

Use quotation marks to note shorter works such as magazine or newspaper articles, short stories, episodes of TV shows, and so on.

➤ The *Murphy Brown* episode called "Murphy Meets the President" is my favorite.

➤ The article "How to Help Your Child Learn to Read" published in the *Transcript* is invaluable.

Titles: Quotation Marks, Italics, Capitalization

- Enclose in quotation marks titles of short works that are not part of a collection, poems, short stories, articles, songs, essays, episodes of radio and television shows, and subdivisions of a book.

  ➤ "When Lilacs Last in the Dooryard Bloom'd" is a poem about the death of Abraham Lincoln.

- Italicize (underline) titles of large works such as books, periodicals, films, television or radio shows, works of visual art, plays, poems published separately as books.

  ➤ *Leaves of Grass* is probably Whitman's most widely circulated collection of poetry.

- Capitalize the first word, the last word, and all other words in a title *except* coordinating conjunctions, articles (*a, an, the*), and prepositions of four letters or less.

  ➤ *Death of a Salesman*

  ➤ *Two Years Before the Mast*

  ➤ *Faulkner: A Biography*

CHECKLIST 26

30b Other Rules for Italics

LETTERS OR WORDS REFERRED TO AS OBJECTS Italicize or underline letters or words used as letters or words.

➤ Remember to cross that *t* and to dot that *i*.

➤ It seems as if every other word she uses is either *like* or *you know*.

TERMS ABOUT TO BE FORMALLY DEFINED Italicize or underline terms if you are about to define them. Remember to put the definition in quotation marks.

➤ The verb *vex* means "to puzzle."

NAMES OF SHIPS AND VEHICLES Italicize or underline the names of ships and vehicles.

➤ Lindbergh's *Spirit of St. Louis* now hangs in the Smithsonian.

➤ The *Flying Cloud* sails out of Tortola.

FOREIGN WORDS AND PHRASES Italicize or underline foreign words and phrases not yet considered part of English, and set off their translation (if given) with quotation marks.

➤ My *compagnon de voyage* was so amusing that the hours on the train flew by.

➤ Visitors to Quebec should take time to review their French—in particular, street signs such as *Arrête* ("Stop").

30c Abbreviations

Use abbreviations sparingly and only when you are sure your readers will understand what you are referring to. Increasingly, abbreviations are accepted as alternate forms of longer terms, and, thus, they are written without spaces or periods between the letters. This practice is especially common when abbreviations are composed of all capital letters (such as acronyms), capital-letter abbreviations of technical terms (*DOS* for "disk operating system"), and names of agencies (*FBI*) and organizations (*NATO*).

To use a less widely known abbreviation throughout a paper, write out the full name for your first reference and immediately follow it with its abbreviation in parentheses.

➤ The Federal Trade Commission (FTC) was established in 1914.

APPROPRIATE ABBREVIATIONS

1. Titles used before and after names are appropriate and can be used freely.

   ➤ Mr.

   ➤ Ms.

   ➤ Rev.

   ➤ Jr.

   ➤ M.B.A. or MBA

   Do not use titles when you are citing. Say, "As Kennedy says," not "As Dr. Kennedy says."

2. Common abbreviations of time and measurement are acceptable and can be used freely.

   ➤ B.C.E. or BCE

   ➤ C.E. or CE

   ➤ a.m. or A.M.

   ➤ 3:00 p.m. or 3:00 P.M.

   ➤ no. (when followed by a specific figure)

3. Use capital letters for common acronyms. Acronyms of three letters or more are customarily written without periods.

   ➤ IBM

   ➤ YMCA

   ➤ PBS

INAPPROPRIATE ABBREVIATIONS   Do not ordinarily abbreviate the following:

1. Personal names

   ➤ ~~Steve~~ *Stephen*

   ➤ ~~Hal~~ *Harold*

2. Days of the week, month of the year, and holidays

   ➤ Classes do not meet on ~~Dec.~~ *December* 25.

3. Names of academic subjects

➤ I am taking ~~econ, poly sci~~, and English.
   economics, political science,

4. Names of most states and countries (*Washington, D.C.,* and the *USA* being exceptions) in an academic paper

➤ She lives in ~~PA~~ during the summer.
   Pennsylvania

5. Divisions of a written text (like chapter and page)

➤ The poem is cited in ~~chap. one~~ on ~~p.~~ 3.
   chapter 1   page

30d Numbers

UP TO NINETY-NINE   Spell out numbers of one or two words, unless there are several numbers within a sentence. For numbers requiring three or more words, use numerals.

➤ twenty

➤ 120

➤ fifty-five

➤ 155

➤ Enrollment figures show that we have 910 returning freshman, 100 transfer students, and 30 graduate students.

The numbers "100" "30" are not spelled out because there are several numbers in this sentence.

AT THE BEGINNING OF SENTENCES   If a sentence begins with a number, either spell out the number or, better, reword the sentence.

➤ ~~150~~ species of water lily are found in the swamp.
   One hundred fifty

or

➤ The pond is home to 150 species of water lily.

USED FOR CLARITY   Use numbers, even in nontechnical writing, to specify exactness in such things as pages and divisions of texts (*page 12*), addresses (*1600 Pennsylvania Avenue*), dates (*May 22, 1978*), time (*9:45 a.m.*), and measurements (*95 percent*).

In dealing with the many special cases, remember to be consistent within your own paper.

31 The Hyphen and Spelling

31a The Hyphen [-]

A hyphen is used to form compound adjectives or compound nouns and with words formed by adding a capital letter.

➤ in-laws

➤ H-bomb

Use a hyphen to show that two or more words are being used as a single adjective before a noun. But when a compound adjective follows a noun, the hyphen is often not used.

➤ an IBM-compatible computer

➤ a computer that is IBM compatible

Use a hyphen to prevent misreading and awkward constructions.

➤ a little-used printer

➤ un-ionized particles

➤ re-covered book

Use a hyphen with certain prefixes

➤ self-sacrifice

➤ ex-president

➤ all-inclusive

➤ quasi-judicial

Note that some compound words (like *real estate*) are written as two words, others (like *manic-depressive*) are hyphenated, while still others (like *fainthearted*) are one word. It is best to rely on a dictionary or spell checker.

Use a hyphen when writing out compound numbers and fractions.

➤ One-fourth of the class graduated with honors.

➤ Numbers from twenty-one to ninety-nine should be hyphenated.

If you choose to divide a word at the end of a line, be sure to hyphenate it between syllables. Check a dictionary whenever you are unsure of how to divide a word. Do not hyphenate the last word of a line; transpose the entire word to the last line. If part of a compound term falls at the end of the line, hyphenate between words, not between syllables.

Note: Word processing programs allow writers to include different types of hyphens. See pages 91–92 for a discussion.

31b   Spelling Rules

Correct spelling is important on final drafts. Even if you are a good speller, be sure to run the spell checker before submitting your paper to either your peers or your teacher. Proofread your paper carefully, remembering to see if you have used words such as *their* and *there* correctly, for a spell checker cannot tell if you have used the wrong word. Finally, make frequent use of your dictionary.

Here are a few spelling pointers to keep in mind:

1. Use *i* before *e* except after *c*, or when sounding like *ay* as in *neighbor* or *weigh*.

   ➤ believe

   ➤ receive

   ➤ sleigh

   EXCEPTIONS   either, seize, height, foreign

2. Words that end in a silent *e* usually drop the *e* when a suffix is added if the suffix begins with a vowel. If the suffix begins with a consonant, however, retain the final *e*.

   ➤ believe, believable

   ➤ achieve, achievement

   EXCEPTIONS   judgment, changeable, argument

3. The root word doesn't change if it is preceded by a prefix.

   ➤ misshapen, disbelief, excommunicate

4. British and American spellings differ for some words.

➤ theater (American), theatre (British)

➤ honor (American), honour (British)

➤ realize (American), realise (British)

➤ canceled (American), cancelled (British)

In your paper, use American spelling throughout, except when you are quoting from British sources, in which case you *must* retain the spellings of the original source.

Refer to the rules below when forming plurals:

1. Form the plural of most nouns by adding -*s* to the noun. Add an -*es* to nouns that end in -*ch*, -*s*, -*sh*, and -*x*.

➤ sailboat, sailboats

➤ church, churches

2. Form the plural of most words that end in *y* by changing the *y* to *i* and adding -*es*, except when the *y* is preceded by a vowel. Just add -*s* to proper names ending in *y*.

➤ variety, varieties

➤ donkey, donkeys

➤ Mary, Marys

3. Form the plural of most words ending in *o* by adding -*s*. However, if the *o* is preceded by a consonant, add -*es*.

➤ radio, radios

➤ potato, potatoes

4. Add an -*s* to the main word of a hyphenated compound word to form its plural.

➤ mothers-in-law

➤ jacks-of-all-trade

5. Words that are derived from other languages sometimes retain the plural of the original language.

➤ chateau, chateaux

➤ lied, lieder

31c Improving Your Spelling

Determine how you can best improve your spelling. Different people learn spelling in different ways. Some find that saying a word out loud and then writing it down helps. Others find that doing a spell check and then mentally sounding out the correct word before directing the computer to insert the word can help. Still other people like to develop mnemonic devices, or memory aids, such as these: *principal* ends in *pal* because the princi*pal* is your *pal*; *independent* has *depend* in it.

One suggestion is to keep a log of your frequently misspelled words. Do not include difficult words with which everyone has trouble. Rather, start with basic words that you have trouble spelling. Note any patterns in the errors you make.

Note: Many word-processing programs, including Microsoft® Word 6.0, allow you to add words to a customized dictionary as you run the spell checker.

31d Frequently Misspelled Words

You may find it helpful to memorize a list of frequently misspelled words, such as the following:

absence	appearance	changeable	decision
academic	appropriate	characteristic	definitely
accidentally	argument	chosen	descendant
accommodate	arithmetic	column	describe
accomplish	arrangement	commitment	description
accumulate	ascend	committed	despair
achievement	athlete	committee	desperate
acknowledge	athletics	comparative	develop
acquaintance	attendance	competitive	dictionary
acquire	audience	conceivable	disappear
across	basically	conference	disappoint
address	beginning	conferred	disastrous
aggravate	believe	conqueror	dissatisfied
all right	benefited	conscience	eighth
a lot	Britain	conscientious	eligible
altogether	bureau	conscious	embarrass
amateur	business	courteous	eminent
among	cafeteria	criticism	emphasize
analyze	calendar	criticize	entirely
answer	candidate	curiosity	environment
apparently	cemetery	dealt	equivalent

especially	irrelevant	phenomenon	schedule
exaggerated	irresistible	physically	secretary
exhaust	knowledge	picnicking	seize
existence	laboratory	playwright	separate
experience	legitimate	politics	sergeant
extraordinary	license	practically	several
extremely	lightning	precede	siege
familiar	loneliness	precedence	similar
fascinate	maintenance	preference	sincerely
February	maneuver	preferred	sophomore
foreign	mathematics	prejudice	subtly
forty	mischievous	primitive	succeed
fourth	necessary	privilege	surprise
friend	noticeable	probably	temperature
government	occasion	proceed	thorough
grammar	occasionally	professor	tragedy
guard	occur	prominent	transferred
guidance	occurred	pronunciation	truly
harass	occurrence	quiet	unnecessarily
height	optimistic	quite	until
humorous	original	receive	usually
illiterate	outrageous	recommend	vacuum
immediately	pamphlet	reference	vengeance
incredible	parallel	referred	villain
indefinitely	particularly	religion	weird
indispensable	pastime	repetition	whether
inevitable	performance	restaurant	writing
infinite	permissible	rhythmical	
intelligence	perseverance	rhythm	
interesting	perspiration	roommate	

GRAMMAR INDEX

INDEX

Entries in *italic* appear in the Usage Glossary (pages 110–22).
Entries in **boldface** appear in the Glossary of Computer-
Based Writing Terms (pages 189–92).

GLOSSARY OF COMPUTER-BASED WRITING TERMS

ASCII (pronounced "ass-key"; originally an acronym for the American Standard Code for Information Interchange). A widely accepted code for assigning numbers to the letters of the alphabet. ASCII files contain only text, with no formatting information, and thus can be easily moved between different programs.

Baud. The speed at which data (including text) can be transmitted, normally over a telephone line using a modem.

Block. A word processing operation in which a section (or block) of text is marked in order to perform an operation on it like deleting it or moving it.

Browser. Software such as Netscape designed for reading through vast amounts of material available on the World Wide Web.

Bullet. A graphical character (typically ●) usually placed before each item in an unnumbered list.

Center. To place text halfway between the left and right margins.

Customizing. The act of changing the default settings and switches inside a software program.

Default. The predefined settings that a program assumes unless instructed otherwise.

Directory. A listing of the files on a disk, collected in one specific area. Subdirectories are collections of files organized under other directories or subdirectories.

Elite. 10-point type—that is, type $\frac{5}{36}$ of an inch tall and traditionally $\frac{1}{12}$ of an inch wide (called 12 pitch)—providing 12 characters to the linear inch.

Em dash. A solid dash the equivalent of the width of the letter *M*. (On a typewriter, two hyphens would be used instead.)

File. The computer's means of organizing blocks of information under a single name. Early computer systems required users to work with files on a constant basis—copying them, renaming them, deleting them, and so forth. Newer, more user-friendly computer systems automate much of this file handling.

File transfer protocol (FTP). A widely used service provided by the Internet for transferring files from one computer to another. With the emergence of the World Wide Web, FTP functions are now largely integrated within browser software.

Fixed fonts. Character sets like those found on typewriters, where each letter, number, punctuation mark, symbol, and space occupies the same width as every other character.

Flush left and flush right. A command that aligns text on the left or right margin, respectively.

Flush right. See *Flush left and flush right.*

Font. All the characters of a given size and design of type.

Footer. Text, with or without a page number, that appears below the bottom margin of all pages or of every other page.

Format. (1) To prepare a blank disk for receiving information; (2) to organize the layout of a printed page, especially regarding size, style, type, margins, and so forth.

Gopher. A system of menus that makes character-based materials at one location available to users worldwide via the Internet. Gopher has been largely superseded by Web pages.

Gutter. In a bound book, the inner margin of a page from printing area to binding.

Hanging margin (also called **hanging indent**). A paragraph style in which the first line begins flush left and all subsequent lines are indented (as in this glossary and in a standard "Works Cited" section).

Hard (nonbreaking) hyphen. A hyphen that, for the purpose of line breaks, attaches itself to the following character.

Hard (nonbreaking) space. A space that, for the purpose of line breaks, attaches itself to the following character.

Header. Text, with or without a page number, that appears above the top margin of all pages or of every other page.

Home page. On the World Wide Web, a file site set up by an individual or institution that directs people to other relevant information about that individual or institution. As such, a home page acts like a title page and a table of contents.

HTML (an acronym for Hypertext Markup Language). A basic system for embedding commands into an ASCII file to display it and related pictures as a hypertext document on the World Wide Web.

Hypertext documents. Screens of online textual and graphical information connected by multiple links. The hypertext version of a standard literary work would have a wealth of secondary information about the work and the author all linked to the primary text; hypertext fiction would have multiple narrative paths much like an interactive adventure game.

Internet. The worldwide interconnection of networks using a basic protocol for the transmission of data. The Internet provides for electronic mail and other forms of information sharing.

Justified. A margin where each line is flush with the line above it; it is created by adjusting the space between words.

Landscape. A rectangular page that is wider than it is tall, as in a typical landscape painting.

Leading (pronounced "led-ing"). The amount of space between lines of type.

Listserv. A program for distributing electronic mail to all people who belong to a particular group. A single mail message sent to the group at the Listserv is automatically distributed to everyone who belongs to that group. In most cases, users can automatically subscribe and unsubscribe to groups by communicating directly with the Listserv program.

Local area network (LAN; also called **ethernet network).** A system in which computers are directly linked together in a single room, office, or building so that they can share files, hard-disk space, and printers.

Log in. To inform a network program that you are online and ready to send and receive information.

Newsgroups. A formal collection of groups organized via Listserv programs; a colorful, informal part of the Internet that permits users with special interests (on almost anything) to communicate with each other by posting personal mail messages to a common electronic bulletin board. There are various software programs that allow individuals to subscribe to individual newsgroups and thus to display automatically recent postings to that group from across the world.

Orphan and widow. A single line of a paragraph that prints on a page by itself and, hence, looks disconnected from its "home." A widow is that last line of a paragraph printed as the first line of a page; an orphan is the first line of a paragraph printed as the last line of a page.

Paragraph margin. The left margin for the first line of a paragraph.

Pica. 12-point type—that is, type ⅙ of an inch tall and traditionally ¹⁄₁₀ of an inch wide (called 10 pitch)—providing 10 characters to the linear inch.

Point. The size of individual characters in a font, with 72 points equal to 1 inch. The standard typing font is 12 points.

Portrait. A rectangular page that is taller than it is wide, as in a typical portrait painting.

Proportional spacing. A feature that assigns differing amounts of space to different characters—for example, *i* takes up less space than *w*.

Ragged margin. An uneven right-hand or left-hand margin, the result of a word processing program's use of a set space between all words.

Sans serif. A typeface without cross strokes at the end of characters (this is sans serif type).

Serif. A typeface with cross strokes at the end of characters (this is serif type).

Soft hyphen. A temporary hyphen used to split a word between lines.

Template file. A "master file," analogous to a printed form, with preset information and questions designed to be completed on many different occasions. As with a printed form, one normally works with a copy of a template file, not the original.

Typeface. The design features common to a complete family of fonts.

URL (an acronym for Uniform Resource Locator). The official description and address of a resource on the Internet.

Usenet. A largely informal arrangement for the sharing of "news" on thousands of different topics among discussion groups set up all over the world. Usenet makes all these discussions available in a single site.

Widow. See *Orphan and widow.*

Wide area network (WAN). The linking of LANs over large distances.

World Wide Web. A system by which much of the information on the Internet is linked together, enabling users to jump transparently from one item and physical location to another.

WYSIWYG (pronounced "wizzywig"; an acronym for What You See Is What You Get). A feature of a word processing program that displays on screen essentially what a document will look like when printed.